TIGER! TIGER!

TIGER! TIGER!

Stories of the Big Cat

Introduction by

Zai Whitaker

talking CUB

An Imprint of Speaking Tiger Books

TALKING CUB
Published by Speaking Tiger Books LLP
125A, Ground Floor, Shahpur Jat,
Near Asiad Village, New Delhi - 110 049

Published in Talking Cub by Speaking Tiger Books in paperback in 2024

ISBN: 978-93-5447-954-0
eISBN: 978-93-5447-953-3

10 9 8 7 6 5 4 3 2 1

Typeset in Lora by Jojy Philip
Printed at: Impressions Printing & Packaging Ltd., Noida

Contents

Introduction Zai Whitakar ix

Tiger in a Typhoon Hugh Allen 1

Drought-stricken Land Dhan Gopal Mukherji 22

Timothy Ruskin Bond 33

The Pipal Pani Tiger Jim Corbett 41

The Tyger William Blake 61

The Hungry Tiger of Oz Ruth Plumly Thompson 63

The Tiger Whisperer Anjana Basu 80

THE Art of Hunting Dhan Gopal Mukherji 98

The Tiger and the Woodcutter William Frederick Travers O'Connor 118

Tiger and Elephant James McIntyre 127

The Palki and the Tiger Maharani Sunity Devi 129

Eyes of the Tiger Bulbul Sharma 136

The Home of the Tigers S. Eardley-Wilmot 143

The Foolish Tiger Flora Annie Steel 156

The Tiger Ella Wheeler Wilcox 161

To See a Tiger Ruskin Bond 163

Tiger, Tiger, Who Are You Aditi De 168

The Jackals and the Tiger
William Frederick Travers O'Connor 179

Padmini Valmik Thapar 185

The Rise and Fall of the Emerald Tigers
Raghu Chundawat 198

'I Want to Be a Man-eater' Ranjit Lal 205

The Tigress Prathibha Nandakumar 222

About the Authors 224

Acknowledgements 232

Introduction

ZAI WHITAKER

Tiger! Tiger! is certainly burning bright because it takes us through a whole range of tiger experiences—from storyland to true tales, from their behaviour and natural history, to poetry and ancient folklore.

India and tigers are practically synonymous. Often when we tell people in other countries that we are from India, they want to talk about tigers (or elephants). Tigers are a big part of our lives and culture. Apart from the many tigers in religion and legends, there's the good old Tiger Balm for headaches and other aches and pains; there are fighters like the Tamil Tigers; the actor Tiger Shroff; and of course every third dog is named Tiger! (Well, slight exaggeration maybe...) And haven't we all nervously recited

William Blake's 'The Tyger' at some point in school?

Why is the tiger such an icon? Because it projects all the 'right' characteristics and qualities we admire and are in awe of. It is big, bold, beautiful, and courageous: what a marvellous animal it is really! Throughout its range, from Tibet and Thailand to India and Indonesia, myth, legend and contemporary writing feature this extraordinary animal. And this collection that you are holding in your hands will take us even closer to it. Let's look at some of the ways the book does this, and enjoy the anticipation before reading it. *Tiger! Tiger!* is going to be a treat, especially for those of you who are interested in wildlife, the environment, and conservation.

I read this book by jumping from story to story as per my fancy. My first reads were the natural history pieces, starting with Valmik Thapar, our world-renowned tiger conservationist who has played an important role in a number of studies, surveys, and in adding to our knowledge about the species. He has worked closely with another tiger legend, Fateh Singh, a Field Director stationed at Ranthambore Tiger Reserve in Rajasthan for many years, learning about this animal. Studying the behaviour and natural history of an animal is an important step towards conserving it because it tells us about its 'basic needs', such as territory, food, vegetation and the geographical features it prefers. Valmik accompanied Fateh Singh on many of these forays, and his first-hand accounts in his many tiger books are fascinating to read. In his essay 'Padmini', he describes a meeting between Fateh and a tigress with five cubs; the former has climbed on to a branch at her approach, and is looking down at her. And being the passionate photographer that he was, he couldn't resist clicking, which caught Padmini's attention: 'On the first click of the camera, Padmini made a threatening charge, stopping directly under the branch where Fateh sat. For a brief moment, the thought of man and tiger confronting each other on the same branch crossed Fateh's mind. But tigers very rarely climb trees, unlike other members of the cat family...'

This is the best way to learn about wildlife—through the acute, scientific, unexaggerated observations of naturalists. Another of this ilk is Jim Corbett, whose 'The Pipal Pani Tiger' is included in this collection. Jim Corbett's name is synonymous with tigers. He is from an earlier generation of naturalists—the naturalist-hunters—who shot tigers for sport as well as to eradicate man-eaters near villages and towns. Corbett's language, powers of observation, and love for our country, makes him a star in the world of Indian natural history. While reading him, we must remember that in his lifetime, hunting was an accepted 'sport' and the numbers of animals were much, much higher.

The other two authors included in this book who also fall into this category are Sir S. Eardley-Wilmot and Hugh Allen. As an added bonus, their fascinating pieces from earlier times come with lovely archaic words like *scatter-gun*, *dust-shot*, and *shewed*. And of course, *the men*, *the boys*, and *natives* (grrrr....)!

There are tiger-centric folktales, great for individual readings or read-alouds. The clever woodcutter circumvents a nasty tiger, and a clever jackal does the same (jackals come in for a lot of bad press in folktales). 'The Palki and the Tiger' features a 'Bengalee' police officer who is out to catch a murderer, but his mission is delayed by a tiger. It's a lovely, quirky tale with a happy ending. Bulbul Sharma's story 'Eyes of the Tiger' also has a happy ending—a safe bedtime read unlike Anjana Basu's 'The Tiger Whisperer', which must be read in the broad daylight for sure!

There's lovely language from much-read stories we can never tire of, like 'Timothy' and 'To See a Tiger', both by our own Bond (Ruskin, not James). The first is a classic twist to the (tiger's) tale, and the second has gems of language which, again, are vintage Bond. The loud frog chorus sounds like an 'old boys' reunion', the streams are moon-green, there are shady glades of sal and shisham trees.

Being interested in education, I found 'The Rise and Fall of the Emerald Tigers' by Raghu Chundawat fascinating. As with any good education system, the mother teaches her cubs to thrive in the world, including catching a fawn alive and allowing them to practice with it (eek, but each to their own). One ambitious mother-teacher even offers tree-climbing lessons, though this isn't a natural activity for tigers. There seem to be defined markers and levels in tiger-school, like in a Montessori program! In 'Drought-Stricken Land', Dhan Gopal Mukherji uses fiction as his tiger-education theme. The mother-tigress Bagni is determined to make a tiger of her cub, and discourages him from hunting man or his animals.

Given the splendid animals that they are, tigers and tigresses have naturally generated beautiful forms of art and craft, music and poetry. The selection of poetry in this collection spans William Blake's 'The Tyger', to contemporary author Prathibha Nandakumar's 'The Tigress'. Blake's peep into the soul of the tiger, and his question 'Did he who made the Lamb make thee?' is timeless, capturing as it does the fantastical beauty and power of this animal. Nandakumar's poem is about a thoroughly brow-beaten tigress in a circus. In my mind, her plight encompasses the state of the dancing bears on the streets, the snakecharmers, the monkeys, parakeets, elephants...and all the other cultural and religious events that make use of 'trained' animals. It's also a powerful poem.

And what's a tiger anthology without some humour thrown in? This comes from Ranjit Lal, the naturalist who combines information, lovely descriptions, and humour, in his endearing stories. The story here, 'I Want to Be a Man-eater', is about a bold little tiger cub who wants to be a man-eater. His entry is memorable: 'the most gorgeous, orange and black tiger cub swaggered out, looking slightly drunk, it had to be said...' You can read the rest; I won't be a spoiler!

Tiger! Tiger! brings the tiger to life for us in a range of genres, perspectives and historical periods: from the old hunting days to current wildlife studies. As I said, it's a treat, both for the classroom as well as the home.

Tiger in a Typhoon

HUGH ALLEN

It was 1955 and the hot weather nearly at an end. That year the heat had been appalling, and now, at the end of June, Babs and I were feeling the effects and scanning the skies each day for signs of rain. Around the estate everything was tinder-dry, and with the earth in the fields like lumps of iron it was difficult to get on with preparations for sowing.

The rains were overdue, but the papers had at last told us that the monsoon had broken over southern India. All being well it should reach us within a few days.

Now that the rains were so close it was time to inspect the nullahs and ravines which drain water from the land and lead it down to the Denwa River. At the start of the rains these often get clogged with fallen trees and the accumulated debris of the year. If this debris is allowed to collect trouble can follow: loose dams form quickly and then the force of the current soon jams everything into a solid and hard-to-move mass. That can mean flooded fields for perhaps the whole of the rains.

Another thing to watch for is the poachers' fish-traps which always appear just before the rains start. These are low, semi-circular walls of loose stone built across the nullahs with a small opening to channel the fish. Dams in miniature; but small as they are, they soon collect debris and often cause a great deal of flooding if they are not found and demolished before the first waters swirl down to the river. One of the poachers' favourite spots, and also one where many natural dams build up, is the big nullah.

This is always the first place I go to when inspecting before the rains. Sure enough there was a half-completed fish-trap before I had gone a quarter of a mile. No one was near it when I came up, but farther along and round a bend I could hear voices and the sounds of men collecting stones from the nullah bed. I climbed the bank and waited behind a tree.

There were two of them, and I let them get right back with their loads before I pounced. They were very sheepish and apologetic—as indeed they should have been; this nonsense has always been a sort of annual fixture and with monotonous regularity I catch the same men year after year. While they were knocking the wall down I told them that they could rebuild it after the debris in the nullah had been swept away. They had known to start with that this permission was theirs simply by coming to ask for it; but as it is much easier to build a wall on dry sand than when water is racing down the nullah, the 'catch-me-if-you-can' tactics are always well worth trying.

When the last stone had been thrown down, Matchu, the elder of the two men, said, 'You want to see the tiger's kill?'

To hear him mention that again surprised me. While the wall was still standing, and while pleas were still being made for it to remain so, there had been a casual reference to a tiger's kill which they said they had found on their way to the nullah. The sudden introduction of that into the middle of the pleading had sounded so fishy that I took no notice; red herring of the same sort had been drawn across my path before. And not always without success, for on two occasions I had set off at once to investigate news of a very similar kind. In the heat of the moment the fish-traps had been forgotten; then—hours later—when nothing had been found and it seemed likely that I had been chasing a wild goose, I hadn't had the heart to send the culprits back to demolish their wall as I could not be sure I'd been had for a mug and that the poachers were not after all honest fellows only trying to be helpful.

'Where is the kill?' I asked. I was interested now and ready to believe that there might be something in the story. With the fish-trap down, they had nothing to gain by sending me off on a false scent.

Matchu pointed along the nullah: 'It's not very far down there, up on the left bank.' Then he added: 'We think it might be the Mograwallah.'

That was interesting indeed. The Mograwallah was a well-known cattle-thief which had been proscribed for more than a year. I motioned them to go ahead and we set off down the nullah. After following it for some three hundred yards we climbed up the bank and then struck off through ground thickly covered with withered bushes and small trees. A short walk brought us up to a patch of thick jungle. Matchu pointed towards it with a finger to his lips. We went in quietly and after twenty yards Matchu pointed again. The kill was a cow which had been dragged half under a spread of lantana and a heavy meal had been eaten off the hindquarters. I was glad to see that it was not one of ours.

From where we were standing it was not far to the pool in the nullah, at this time of the year the only water for a long way around. When I had thanked the men for showing me the kill I sent them away and then set off to the pool to see what I could find. The tiger's pugmarks were all round the water.

Some of them were fresh, but a lot more showed that the tiger had been using the pool for perhaps two weeks; from the signs he was a nice animal and might well be the Mograwallah.

I had not been to the pool for quite a while, but two weeks is a longish time for a tiger to hang about and I was wondering why I had not heard of him. Half an hour later I had found two more kills in that same patch of jungle. These were older than the first one, and both had been finished by hyenas which had scattered bones over a wide area. Like a lot of other cattle-killers, it looked as though the Mograwallah never returned to a kill after the first feed.

The three dead cows so close together and near the pool suggested that this tiger was unlikely to leave until after the rains had broken. He was obviously getting all he wanted to eat, and he was getting it from the hundreds of straying cattle now wandering the estate. During the hot months of the year these cattle are a perpetual nuisance; and for several reasons, all of them wrapped up in the Indian attitude towards cows, little or nothing can be done to keep them off the land.

The nuisance is considerable and begins each year as soon as the crops are cut. By this time the weather is warming up and the village pastures are already heavily over-grazed, so what the cattle owners do is drive their animals right out to fend for themselves. No one is in charge of them and they wander where they will; as the hot weather advances and the grazing grows even scarcer, the cattle have to keep feeding both by day and night just to stay alive. Until the rains revive the grass, none of them ever goes home for the good reason that there is nothing to eat there at all.

Sooner or later all these cattle wander to the estate where they try to stay. Along the river banks the pastures are naturally good and not overgrazed if we can stop it. But what a job trying to keep these strays away! The local cattle pound holds only forty animals and we have to deal with hundreds a day; but even if the pound held them all it would still be no solution. The cattle owners keep a wary eye cocked for anyone leading their animals to the pound; whenever our men appear with a bunch of strays, word spreads rapidly and there is likely to be a fight. To this state of affairs officialdom merely shrugs its shoulders; the problems posed by Indian cows are so many that no one even tries to solve them. The only thing to do then is keep driving the strays away; but to employ men simply for this is not practical and so there are always scores of cattle wandering the estate.

A paradise for a cattle-killing tiger, and what this one was doing was simply staying put and picking off a cow whenever he was hungry. If he kept to the straying cattle I couldn't care less; but with our own herds wandering the estate too, and with small boys in charge of them, something would have to be done to end the Mograwallah's career.

Two days later he killed again. The victim was another stray cow which he took at the top of the path coming up from the pool. Once more he had dragged the body into the same patch of jungle he had taken the others to. On the morning I found this kill we'd had the first shower of the monsoon which had left the ground soft and the dry leaves sodden. The tiger had eaten a heavy meal and was not likely to be very far away. It was a good chance, for with the ground just right for stalking it might be possible to find him asleep.

It was another of those occasions when the tiger found me first and handed out a fright. It may be that I woke him suddenly or he might have been awake all the time and watching me from behind some bushes. Whatever the truth was he gave no chance but sprang away with a roar when he decided that I was too close to be friendly.

On my way home for lunch I saw that the black clouds were gathering again. At two o'clock the rain started, heavy stuff which left no doubt that the monsoon had at last arrived. To sit for a tiger in a deluge is neither sensible nor pleasant so I cancelled the machan I had told Bhutu to build.

Besides, this tiger would now move off when the rain drove the straying cattle back to the shelter of their mangers.

The rain went on all night and there was no sign of it letting up by dawn the next morning.

An hour later it was still very dark for the skies were a lowering mass of black, angry-looking clouds tinged with an ugly yellow. The rain started to come down harder and thunder began to growl overhead; by mid-morning the barometer on the veranda was as low as I had ever seen it.

The weather now looked ugly indeed and there was something about the sky that alarmed me; overhead the clouds seemed to be boiling as they lashed out the rain. A few seconds later I had forgotten them when, above the smashing of the deluge, I suddenly heard the roar of the rising river four hundred yards away. It was a sound that sent me hurrying back to my raincoat and gumboots.

The river of course always rises when the rains start and it often rises fast. But this rise was too sudden and suggested abnormal conditions which had not been there when I visited the river bank fifteen minutes before.

When I reached the river the roar of the racing waters was deafening. Far upstream I could see nothing of the causeway that takes the main road across the riverbed; in its place was a frothing, muddy-white line stretching from bank to bank. That meant a rise of nearly twenty feet in perhaps as many minutes: somewhere up in the mountains about Pachmarhi where the Denwa has its source, there must have been a lot more rain than even we'd had. After watching the river for some minutes I squelched across to the big nullah.

I found the water here already over the banks and flooding the land on both sides; the current down the centre was like a raging millstream. From force of habit I started to splash through the water as near to the bank as I could judge.

I was looking for the obstruction until I realized that there probably was none; the nullah just wasn't big enough to carry away the tons of water falling from the skies.

At three o'clock in the afternoon it was nearly dark and a high wind was rising steadily. The cattle, which had gone out as usual in the morning, had been brought back at midday and put in their shed. After that I had sent all the men back to their quarters; in this weather there was nothing anyone could do outside, and by the signs in the sky we had not yet seen the worst of it. The skies were getting darker, and as the rain pelted down the wind was rising to a high wailing shriek.

The typhoon struck soon after six. There was little warning, though a fiery blast of shattering thunder may have been its herald. A few seconds later the elements went mad and the world was suddenly a howling inferno struck through with violent flashes of vivid violet light. The fury of the wind was frightening. It was roaring through the trees with a speed that appalled and the whole house was shuddering to the screaming impact. Above the deafening roar we could hear loud snaps as branches were torn from the trees and the grinding crashes as forest giants slammed down before the onslaught.

Within fifteen minutes of the first blast the roof of the cowshed was torn off bodily. We heard it start to tear loose, then came the rumble and rattle of falling bricks. Hard behind that rose the frantic cries of terrified cattle and the clatter of stampeding hooves on concrete.

All at once the clatter stopped, bitten off by the wind with alarming suddenness.

As I looked at the damage, the torch was hardly needed. The wreckage was brilliant under the almost continuous lightning. The roof had reared upwards and then levered down one entire longitudinal wall. The debris had fallen on the cattle and three of them were still writhing under a mass of splintered rafters and rubble; of the others there was no sign.

With four men carrying lanterns I set off to look for them. The force of the wind now was such that the driving rain really hurt our bare hands and faces. We had scarcely gone two hundred yards to the north of the house when we were pulled up short. Stretching away into the night was a solid sheet of water. It covered the field in front of us to disappear into the trees fringing the far side; as far as we could see to the right and left of us there was water everywhere flooding up from the nullah.

We turned left and skirted along by the water. Almost at once we found the cattle. They had not gone far and were huddled together under some trees with the water lapping their legs. By now they had calmed down and gave no trouble when the men started to drive them home.

I left the men to it and then set off to find out how bad things really were. The rain was still slashing down, but even so the extent of the flooding from the nullah had come as a shock to me. What about the river? That was a much more formidable force and as I hurried across to it the first tinge of anxiety rose about the safety of the house.

The house is on a part of the estate which is roughly triangular. One side of the triangle is formed by the river. The other side is the nullah which, after running diagonally across the estate, meets the river to form the apex; about the centre of the base, between the river and the nullah, the house stands on a slight rise.

With my head down I turned into the wind and fought towards the river in a straight line. Even today I can recall vividly almost every step of that journey. It was like a waking nightmare with the wind nearly strong enough to lean on as it tore past with its unearthly shriek. Long before I should have reached the river my way was barred by its flooding waters coming to meet me. This was far worse than the nullah; you could see the water creeping up to the thunderous roar coming from behind the line of trees that marked the river bank in the rain-obscured distance.

I was just starting to move on to where the river meets the nullah, three-quarters of a mile from where I was standing, when I caught a sudden flurry of movement across the water in front of me. I switched on the torch quickly. Through the silvery rods of the rain smashing through the beam I saw a pack of wild dogs scampering towards me. They came on and then jumped to the dry land. They were within a few yards and all round me, whimpering and uttering sharp little cries of alarm; for all the notice they took of me I might not have been there.

As I walked on I kept the light sweeping across the waters. After a few minutes I switched it off; the lightning was better, the almost continuous flashes lit the scene around me like daylight.

Not far on from where I had left the wild dogs I saw a small herd of spotted deer, four hinds and a stag, splashing out from a wood which in normal times is a hundred yards from the river; now it was an island of trees. They must have seen me as clearly as I could see them, but they splashed on, away from the greater danger of the rising water. When they had passed only a little way behind me I went on. There was still no sign of the storm abating and the wind was driving the pelting rain as strongly as ever; the thunder was still crashing with scarcely a break. After another fifty yards I stopped again.

This time there was no going on. The waters now were not only on my left but on my right as well, and just in front of me they met. The river and the nullah were now a single sheet of water. For a few moments I just stood still staring at the floods. The danger to the house now was very real. From where I was it was only a quarter of a mile away and the waters were creeping towards it from two sides.

I turned quickly and started back. Almost at once I found myself in another nightmare of a different kind. Across my path there was suddenly a great sounder of pig standing motionless. To get past them I had to skirt to one side in spite of a great throat-tearing shout to move them. Then animals were everywhere. In the flashes from the skies I could see them all around me, some standing still while others moved slowly as though in a dream. I did not know then that we were all on an island only some ten acres in extent which was rapidly growing smaller.

When I got back to the house, Babs had some coffee waiting on the stove. When I had gulped it down I went out again to see the cattle. They had been put in an old and long-disused 'country' shed. The roof was of rough thatch, the sides built of light stakes lashed together with strips of bamboo; the only reason why this was still standing was probably because the wind had no 'push' against its openwork sides.

The cattle were very restless. Now that they were locked up again the collapse of the roof in their old shed was obviously still a vivid memory. They were milling around wildly, barging into one another and crashing against the flimsy sides. If this shed collapsed it would not be the wind but the cattle which pulled it down. But there was nowhere else to put them, the three other sheds were some distance from the house and were already under water when I passed them on my way back.

Half an hour later I went out again. The swollen nullah was now within a hundred yards of the house and the river had swept across the base of the triangle to join it. The area of our island had now shrunk to about three acres—and there was still no sign of the rain stopping.

On my way back to the house I had another look at the cattle. They were still very restless but still safe inside. That hardly seemed to matter now. I was going to give the rain another hour and if it had not stopped then I should let them out to take their chance in the floods.

Some twenty minutes later, as we were sitting in a room at the back of the house, it seemed to me that the rain had suddenly slackened. I got up and went out towards the front veranda. When I reached the door leading to it I stopped and looked out. There was no light outside and none in the room behind me. Beyond the veranda the lightning was vivid, the scene beneath it as light as day. The rain was stopping.

Then, as I stared out at it, a slight movement from the left turned my eyes. A tiger was standing at the end of the veranda. It had been the merest flash of a picture but clear beyond mistake. The lightning flashed again and it was still there.

A moment later I was in the back room grabbing for the rifle. The magazine was full and a torch mounted on the barrel for I had only recently put it down. Back again at the veranda door I peered round. The tiger was still there and I snapped on the light. But he didn't wait a second. As the light hit him he sprang...out of it and away into the night. The bullet I sent after him was wide and smacked into a concrete trough in the garden.

It was the last straw for the cattle. In his flight the tiger streaked past their shed. That was all they needed: a strong whiff of tiger slammed into their nostrils by the wind. They were stampeding wildly before the echoes of the shot died away. There was a violent crash and the shed was matchwood. Then the cattle were out and thundering away snorting with terror.

As the sounds of their flight faded I suddenly realized that the rain had stopped. All at once the main sound of the night was the mighty roar of the river. A good sound now. One that told that the dangers of the floods were over. The river falls just as fast as it rises and that loud booming proclaimed that the waters were receding and racing away to the sea.

What the extent of the damage was I could not even guess, but that was something to worry about in the morning, In the meantime we had to round up the cattle again and somehow bed them down for the rest of the night. That should not take long: they could not have gone far as they would certainly keep to the dry land about the house. That there was also a tiger somewhere in that small area was not really much to worry about. That beast had plenty of troubles of his own, for if ever I had seen a frightened animal it was this tiger when he sprang away from the veranda. For him it had been any port in the worst storm of his life, and he had been on the veranda only because it must have seemed to him the one safe spot in a world suddenly gone mad.

Nor did he in fact give any trouble. The cattle were rounded up safely and left in an open compound at the back of the house. By breakfast time the next morning the river was nearly back in its bed and the sun was shining brightly from a blue sky. When the cattle went out to graze I told the boys in charge of them not to go too far from the house.

After such an exciting night that tiger might be hungry....

Drought-stricken Land

DHAN GOPAL MUKHERJI

Bagni went on teaching her cub. His final training lay in learning those feelings by which an animal knows remote dangers. Though remote, they are just as destructive as the attack by an enemy at hand. What are the remote dangers that threaten a tiger's life? They are fire, flood, drought and disease. A cat has to know them.

February was over. Mother and son moved into the neighbourhood of man. In some parts of India it is the period of migration. From the first of March the dry season rules. The present short spring ended in a heat wave. First, it put its tentacles at the root of saplings, reeds, bamboo, and grass. Then, leaf by leaf the trees lost their brief spring foliage. The sudden burst of fragrance fell upon the land like a storm. Winter's decay was swept aside in a week.

In turn, spring was flung out of existence by the drought. Flowers withered as if poisoned. Leaves turned ashen on boughs. Dust like the finest powder descended layer upon layer on seeds and unborn herbs to hide them from the sun. That which yesterday was panoplied with spring now hid itself under a raiment of dust.

Such a crisis drives the wild ones in two directions. Some go to the depth of the jungle where thick branches of aged trees save the springs from completely drying up, while the rest of the forest-folk go to the land of wide rivers on whose banks men live.

'Civilization follows rivers.' The villages of India dot the banks of her immense streams. There seems to be an ancient understanding between men and beasts. They draw nearer each other oppressed by the common terror of drought bordering on famine. During this particular dry season, Fierce-Face met mankind; also a man-eating tiger.

This man-eater was about sixteen years old, past his prime. His wind was poor. As for his muscles, they could not keep up a long chase after a wild animal of any kind. On the other hand, he had strength enough to pursue and kill domestic animals: such as cows, water buffaloes, sheep and goats. His powers were better than theirs. Every fibre of his body had been exercised, while they had lived their days at a slow pace.

It fell out that one day while he was chasing a cow, its herder stood in his way. The old cat was insane with anger. Without thinking, he chased and killed the wretched fellow. His easy victory over the unarmed biped convinced him that a man is easy to kill.

As the drought grew more and more relentless, bolder became the man-eater. In fact, he settled down to attack men and women and children. He had four legs to their two. He ran faster than they. Their two-footed run was no match for his speed.

The villagers found it dangerous to go out of doors after four in the afternoon. If there were some hardy spirits that did venture out, they left off doing so the moment they realized that there were two more tigers: Fierce-Face and his mother.

These two cats had come to the neighbourhood of man indirectly; for they wanted to live near the broad river whose shores were ornamented with pasture, gardens and huts. The farmers who had seen the three cats thought them to be husband, wife and son! They hated the old murderer with good reason, but their hate of the other two was groundless.

In the meantime, the man-eater felt that the other cats had come to rob him of his single-handed reign of terror.

In order to feel safe, the villagers came to their parched fields with beat of drums, roar of trumpets, and lighted torches. The cringing bipeds had united their forces to meet the triple tiger-menace. No matter how brave, any tiger would run from the thunder of drums and swaying of a dozen torches.

Little Fierce-Face was disturbed. But not his mother. Her discipline grew harsher. She was determined to make a tiger out of him. His cub days must be ended. The rules that she had made had to be obeyed. She insisted on sleep by day and hunt by night. Besides, she refused her son's request to hunt man or his animals. She forced him to live by preying on the wild beasts that had drawn towards man's world of tawny rivers. It was not very easy to pursue many of these creatures, for there was no high grass to conceal the killer. Nor were there plants with leaves to give hiding quarters. In the moonlit hours the plains burnt with bright gold light betraying the movements of the smallest animals.

Yet mother and son disdained hurting man and his cattle. Once they killed a cow by mistake. It was a dark dusty night. By some chance the cowherds had forgotten a cow. This stupid animal had strayed far into the wilderness.

About midnight, Fierce-Face sighted on the bank of the river a crystal shape haloed with moonbeams. It struck awe into his heart. He had never seen a white cow roaming wild before. To him it was a divinity. His instinct urged him to sneak past this apparition of beauty. But something touched the tip of his tail. It was the paw of his guardian. She was saying, 'Attack, or I will strike you.'

He hesitated. Again that slight touch telegraphed to his brain, 'Attack or...'

Suddenly, the cow rose and groaned in anger. With horns ready, she came like a thunderbolt at the four sea-coloured eyes that she had seen. Fierce-Face was touched by terror. But that was nothing compared with the terrifying 'Grr' of his mother. It forced him to leap forward. The dusty moonlit air felt like sprays of topaz-coloured down.

At last he had done it! But the cow was too strong. With one shake of her body she threw him off her shoulder and plunged headlong at the mother. Alas, the tigress was an expert: she dodged by moving aside. Then she leaped at the cow, but missed. Apparently her intention was to make the cub do all the work. He seemed to sense this. He rushed after the fleeing prey roaring like a veteran of the game.

At this stage the bovine saw something that frightened her to a standstill. There was a third tiger standing in the distance. Stupidity, the proverbial quality of cows, led to her undoing. Instead of plunging at the man-eater, who had only come to look, she stopped to think. Before she had taken any decisive step, Fierce-Face was upon her neck.

The mother tiger watched, not her son but the old cat. He was already coming forward to share in the kill.

With a growl for a warning, she charged. The moonlight dripped from her body in silver rain. Claws and teeth began their deadly work. Howls of hate rolled on the river, then struck the sleeping houses and roofs.

In a few minutes the old fellow had learnt that it must be retreat or death. At this point he saw another tiger coming towards him. It was Fierce-Face bringing aid to his mother. This shook his self-confidence. A sharp blow seared his body. He rushed away into the jungle.

This battle led to the man-eater's capture by men. But we must tell the story event by event.

~

On the morrow, the old cat found himself bruised and cut in many places. Not only that, he had bled profusely through one wound. He was forced to heal himself. So he took to eating herbs. And these were not easy to find. Next he needed salt for his diet. Beasts of prey generally get salt from the meat and blood of their kill. He had no strength to get a victim. The only way left for him was to lick the mud of the river, for it was full of salty deposit. For days his diet consisted of mud and a few herbs. Owing to it he was not able to move fast or far.

A glance at the map of India will tell one that the Ganges reaches the sea in the Province of Bengal, the home of Royal Bengal tigers. There the water is full of crocodiles and the long fingers of land full of tigers. The holy river forks out into innumerable mud-red streams. Though the place rarely sees pythons, during the rains of August floods from the north wash down Himalayan serpents many feet long to the jungles of the salt lick. Once there, a tiger rarely forsakes the place. For to the long neck of land come many vegetarian animals to eat salt which prevents diseases such as dropsy. Here, at last, the civilized human beings found it easy to track the man-eater down.

By watching from tree-tops, they made out the state of his health. Man's cunning worked faster than the animal's wisdom. They dug a pit ten feet deep and as many feet square, then covered it with bamboo and luscious twigs. To make it all the more innocent-looking they left a dozen roosters tethered to long strings on top. These crowed or ate grains of rice thrown down from a tree where a man hid. The latter had built a spacious platform where he kept sacks of food both for himself and for the decoys below. From his point of vantage he could see the movements of many animals on the floor of the jungle.

After several days spent in eating salty mud and grass, the man-eater felt very hungry. He needed diet fit for his race. His instinct told him to return to the village to hunt. This was difficult for one tired and worn. He felt hungrier and hungrier; every step that he took seemed to be his last.

It was about eleven in the morning when he was passing near the trap. He heard a rooster crow. He realized at once that it was a barnyard fowl. Thinking that he was drawing close to a village, he tried to hurry in the direction of the noise. He could not walk fast.

At this juncture he heard the roosters crow several times, and his ears told him that the birds were within reach. He ambled on laboriously. It was not long before he was standing near the trap. In the white heat haze caused by the tropical sun the yellow-red birds appeared like woodcocks of the wild. Deceptive colours hung in the air between the cat and the barnyard fowl. Just the same something within him hinted that he had better keep away.

From a tree-top a twig fell, hitting one of the birds. Its wings fluttered; then it screamed in pain. The man-eater surmised that all the birds might fly away, and he was too hungry to let this happen. So he rushed at the feathered fraternity. Then like a sleeper falling in his dreams, he fell—down and down and down...

Suddenly, he struck the bottom of the trap. Though the chickens had fallen with him, he had no desire to eat them. The catastrophe had robbed him of his appetite.

There he lay three days. Instead of killing him the villagers placed him in an iron cage and drove him to the nearest dealer in animals. After selling him, they took the proceeds home. It was distributed evenly among those whose cattle the man-eater had slain.

Timothy

RUSKIN BOND

Timothy, the tiger cub, was discovered by Grandfather on a hunting expedition in the Terai jungle near Dehra.

Grandfather was no shikari, but as he knew the forests of the Siwalik hills better than most people, he was persuaded to accompany the party—it consisted of several Very Important Persons from Delhi—to advise on the terrain and the direction the beaters should take once a tiger had been spotted.

The camp itself was sumptuous—seven large tents (one for each shikari), a dining-tent, and a number of servants' tents. The dinner was very good, as Grandfather admitted afterwards; it was not often that one saw hot-water plates, finger-glasses, and seven or eight courses, in a tent in the jungle! But that was how things were done in the days of the Viceroys... There were also some fifteen elephants, four of them with howdahs for the shikaris, and the others specially trained for taking part in the beat.

The sportsmen never saw a tiger, nor did they shoot anything else, though they saw a number of deer, peacocks, and wild boars. They were giving up all hope of finding a tiger, and were beginning to shoot at jackals, when Grandfather, strolling down the forest path at some distance from the rest of the party, discovered a little tiger about 18 inches long, hiding among the intricate roots of a banyan tree. Grandfather picked him up, and brought him home after the camp had broken up. He had the distinction of being the only member of the party to have bagged any game, dead or alive.

At first the tiger cub, who was named Timothy by Grandmother, was brought up entirely on milk given to him in a feeding bottle by our cook, Mahmoud. But the milk proved too rich for him, and he was put on a diet of raw mutton and cod liver oil, to be followed later by a more tempting diet of pigeons and rabbits.

Timothy was provided with two companions—Toto the monkey, who was bold enough to pull the young tiger by the tail, and then climb up the curtains if Timothy lost his temper; and a small mongrel puppy, found on the road by Grandfather.

At first Timothy appeared to be quite afraid of the puppy, and darted back with a spring if it came too near. He would make absurd dashes at it with his large forepaws, and then retreat to a ridiculously safe distance. Finally, he allowed the puppy to crawl on his back and rest there!

One of Timothy's favourite amusements was to stalk anyone who would play with him, and so, when I came to live with Grandfather, I became one of the favourites of the tiger. With a crafty look in his glittering eyes, and his body crouching, he would creep closer and closer to me, suddenly making a dash for my feet, rolling over on his back and kicking me in delight, and pretending to bite my ankles.

He was by this time the size of a full-grown retriever, and when I took him out for walks, people on the road would give us a wide berth. When he pulled hard on his chain, I had difficulty in keeping up with him. His favourite place in the house was the drawing room, and he would make himself comfortable on the long sofa, reclining there with great dignity, and snarling at anybody who tried to get off.

Timothy had clean habits, and would scrub his face with his paws exactly like a cat. He slept at night in the quarters, and was always delighted at being let out in the morning.

'One of these days,' declared Grandmother in prophetic manner, 'we are going to find Timothy sitting on Mahmoud's bed, and no sign of the cook except his clothes and shoes!'

Of course, it never came to that, but when Timothy was about six months old a change came over him; he grew steadily less friendly. When out for a walk with me, he would try to steal away to stalk a cat or someone's pet Pekinese. Sometimes at night we would hear frenzied cackling from the poultry house, and in the morning there would be feather lying all over the veranda. Timothy had to be chained up more often. And finally, when he began to stalk Mahmoud about the house with what looked like villainous intent, Grandfather decided it was time to transfer him to a zoo.

The nearest zoo was at Lucknow, 200 miles away. Reserving a first-class compartment for himself and Timothy—no one would share a compartment with them—Grandfather took him to Lucknow where the zoo authorities were only too glad to receive as a gift a well-fed and fairly civilized tiger.

About six months later, when my grand-parents were visiting their relatives in Lucknow, Grandfather took the opportunity of calling at the zoo to see how Timothy was getting on. I was not there to accompany him, but I heard all about it when he returned to Dehra.

Arriving at the zoo, Grandfather made straight for the particular cage in which Timothy had been interned. The tiger was there, crouched in a corner, full-grown and with a magnificent striped coat.

'Hello Timothy!' said Grandfather, and, climbing the railing with ease, he put his arm through the bars of the cage.

The tiger approached the bars, and allowed Grandfather to put both hands around his head. Grandfather stroked the tiger's forehead and tickled his ear, and whenever he growled, smacked him across the mouth, which was his old way of keeping him quiet.

He licked Grandfather's hands and only sprang away when a leopard in the next cage snarled at him. Grandfather shooed the leopard away, and the tiger returned to lick his hands; but every now and then the leopard would rush at the bars, and the tiger would slink back to his corner.

A number of people had gathered to watch the reunion when a keeper pushed his way through the crowd and asked Grandfather what he was doing. 'I'm talking to Timothy,' said Grandfather. 'Weren't you here when I gave him to the zoo six months ago?'

'I haven't been here very long,' said the surprised keeper. 'Please continue your conversation. But I have never been able to touch him myself, he is always very bad tempered.'

'Why don't you put him somewhere else?' suggested Grandfather. 'That leopard keeps frightening him. I'll go and see the Superintendent about it.'

Grandfather went in search of the Superintendent of the zoo, but found that he had gone home early; and so, after wandering about the zoo for a little while, he returned to Timothy's cage to say goodbye. It was beginning to get dark.

He had been stroking and slapping Timothy for about five minutes when he found another keeper observing with some alarm. Grandfather recognized him as the keeper who had been there when Timothy had first come to the zoo.

'You remember me,' said Grandfather. 'Now why don't you transfer Timothy to another cage, away from this stupid leopard?'

'But—sir—' stammered the keeper, 'it is not your tiger.'

'I know, I know,' said Grandfather testily. 'I realize he is no longer mine. But you might at least take a suggestion or two from me.'

'I remember your tiger very well,' said the keeper, 'But he died two months ago.'

'Died!' exclaimed Grandfather.

'Yes, sir, of pneumonia. This tiger was trapped in the hills only last month, and he is very dangerous!' Grandfather could think of nothing to say. The tiger was still licking his arm, with increasing relish. Grandfather took what seemed to him an age to withdraw his hand from the cage.

With his face near the tiger's he mumbled, 'Goodnight, Timothy,' and giving the keeper a scornful look, walked briskly out of the zoo.

The Pipal Pani Tiger

JIM CORBETT

Beyond the fact that he was born in a ravine running deep into the foothills and was one of a family of three, I know nothing of his early history.

He was about a year old when, attracted by the calling of a chital hind early one November morning, I found his pugmarks in the sandy bed of a little stream known locally as Pipal Pani. I thought at first that he had strayed from his mother's care, but, as week succeeded week and his single tracks showed on the game paths of the forest, I came to the conclusion that the near approach of the breeding season was an all-sufficient reason for his being alone. Jealously guarded one day, protected at the cost of the parent life if necessary, and set adrift the next, is the lot of all jungle folk; nature's method of preventing inbreeding.

That winter he lived on peafowl, kakar, small pig and an occasional chital hind, making his home in a prostrate giant of the forest felled for no apparent reason, and hollowed out by time and porcupines. Here he brought most of his kills, basking, when the days were cold, on the smooth bole of the tree, where many a leopard had basked before him.

It was not until January was well advanced that I saw the cub at close quarters. I was out one evening without any definite object in view, when I saw a crow rise from the ground and wipe its beak as it lit on the branch of a tree. Crows, vultures and magpies always interest me in the jungle, and many are the kills I have found both in India and in Africa with the help of these birds. On the present occasion the crow led me to the scene of an overnight tragedy. A chital had been killed and partly eaten and, attracted to the spot probably as I had been, a party of men passing along the road, distant some fifty yards, had cut up and removed the remains. All that was left of the chital were a few splinters of bone and a little congealed blood off which the crow had lately made his meal. The absence of thick cover and the proximity of the road convinced me that the animal responsible for the kill had not witnessed the removal and that it would return in due course; so I decided to sit up, and made myself as comfortable in a plum tree as the thorns permitted.

I make no apology to you, my reader, if you differ with me on the ethics of the much-debated subject of sitting up over kills. Some of my most pleasant shikar memories centre round the hour or two before sunset that I have spent in a tree over a natural kill, ranging from the time when, armed with a muzzle-loader whipped round with brass wire to prevent the cracked barrel from bursting, I sat over a langur killed by a leopard, to a few days ago, when with the most modern rifle across my knees, I watched a tigress and her two full-grown cubs eat up the sambur stag they had killed, and counted myself no poorer for not having secured a trophy.

True, on the present occasion there is no kill below me, but, for the reasons given, that will not affect any chance of a shot; scent to interest the jungle folk there is in plenty in the bloodsoaked ground, as witness the old grey-whiskered boar who has been quietly rooting along for the past ten minutes, and who suddenly stiffens to attention as he comes into the line of the blood-tainted wind. His snout held high, and worked as only a pig can work that member, tells him more than I was able to glean from the ground which showed no tracks; his method of approach, a short excursion to the right and back into the wind, and then a short excursion to the left and again back into the wind, each manoeuvre bringing him a few yards nearer, indicates the chital was killed by a tiger. Making sure once and again that nothing worth eating has been left, he finally trots off and disappears from view.

Two chital, both with horns in velvet, now appear and from the fact that they are coming down-wind, and making straight for the blood-soaked spot, it is evident they were witnesses to the overnight tragedy. Alternately snuffing the ground, or standing rigid with every muscle tensed for instant flight, they satisfy their curiosity and return the way they came.

Curiosity is not a human monopoly; many an animal's life is cut short by indulging in it. A dog leaves the verandah, to bark at a shadow, a deer leaves the herd to investigate a tuft of grass that no wind agitated, and the waiting leopard is provided with a meal.

The sun is nearing the winter line when a movement to the right front attracts attention. An animal has crossed an opening between two bushes at the far end of a wedge of scrub that terminates thirty yards from my tree. Presently the bushes at my end part, and out into the open, with never a look to right or left, steps the cub. Straight up to the spot where his kill had been he goes, his look of expectancy giving place to one of disappointment as he realizes that his chital, killed, possibly, after hours of patient stalking, is gone. The splinters of bone and congealed blood are rejected, and his interest centres on a tree stump lately used as a butcher's block, to which some shreds of flesh are adhering. I was not the only one who carried fire arms in these jungles and, if the cub was to grow into a tiger, it was necessary he should be taught the danger of carelessly approaching kills in daylight. A scatter-gun and dust-shot would have served my purpose better, but the rifle will have to do this time; and, as he raises his head to smell the stump, my bullet crashes into the hard wood an inch from his nose. Only once in the years that followed did the cub forget that lesson.

The following winter I saw him several times. His ears did not look so big now and he had changed his baby hair for a coat of rich tawny red with well-defined stripes. The hollow tree had been given up to its rightful owners a pair of leopards, new quarters found in a thick belt of scrub skirting the foothills, and young sambur added to his menu.

On my annual descent from the hills next winter, the familiar pugmarks no longer showed on the game paths and at the drinking places, and for several weeks I thought the cub had abandoned his old haunts and gone further afield. Then one morning his absence was explained for, side by side with his tracks were the smaller and more elongated tracks of the mate he had gone to find. I only once saw the tigers, for the cub was a tiger now, together. I had been out before dawn to try to bag a serow that lived on the foothills, and returning along a fire track my attention was arrested by a vulture, perched on the dead limb of a sal tree.

The bird had his back towards me and was facing a short stretch of scrub with dense jungle beyond. Dew was still heavy on the ground, and without a sound I reached the tree and peered round. One antler of a dead sambur, for no living deer would lie in that position, projected above the low bushes. A convenient moss-covered rock afforded my rubbershod feet silent and safe hold, and as I drew myself erect, the sambur came into full view. The hind quarters had been eaten away and, lying on either side of the kill were the pair, the tiger being on the far side with only his hind legs showing. Both tigers were asleep. Ten feet straight in front, to avoid a dead branch, and thirty feet to the left would give me a shot at the tiger's neck, but in planning the stalk I had forgotten the silent spectator. Where I stood I was invisible to him, but before the ten feet had been covered I came into view and, alarmed at my near proximity, he flapped off his perch, omitting as he did so to notice a thin creeper dependent from a branch above him against which he collided, and came ignominiously to ground. The tigress was up and away in an instant, clearing at a bound the kill and her mate, the tiger not being slow to follow; a possible shot, but too risky with thick jungle ahead where a wounded animal would have all the advantages. To those who have never tried it, I can recommend the stalking of leopards and tigers on their kills as a most pleasant form of sport. Great care should however be taken over the shot, for if the animal is not killed outright, or anchored, trouble is bound to follow.

A week later the tiger resumed his bachelor existence. A change had now come over his nature. Hitherto he had not objected to my visiting his kills but, after his mate left, at the first drag I followed up I was given very clearly to understand that no liberties would in future be permitted. The angry growl of a tiger at close quarters, than which there is no more terrifying sound in the jungles, has to be heard to be appreciated.

Early in March the tiger killed his first full-grown buffalo. I was near the foothills one evening when the agonized bellowing of a buffalo, mingled with the angry roar of a tiger, rang through the forest. I located the sound as coming from a ravine about six hundred yards away. The going was bad, mostly over loose rocks and through thorn bushes, and when I crawled up a steep bluff commanding a view of the ravine the buffalo's struggles were over, and the tiger nowhere to be seen. For an hour I lay with finger on trigger without seeing anything of the tiger. At dawn next morning I again crawled up the bluff, to find the buffalo lying just as I had left her. The soft ground, torn up by hoof and claw, testified to the desperate nature of the struggle and it was not until the buffalo had been hamstrung that the tiger had finally succeeded in pulling her down, in a fight which had lasted from ten to fifteen minutes. The tiger's tracks led across the ravine and, on following them up, I found a long smear of blood on a rock, and, a hundred yards further on, another smear on a fallen tree. The wound inflicted by the buffalo's horns was in the tiger's head and sufficiently severe to make the tiger lose all interest in the kill, for he never returned to it.

Three years later the tiger, disregarding the lesson received when a cub (his excuse may have been that it was the close season for tigers), incautiously returned to a kill, over which a zamindar and some of his tenants were sitting at night, and received a bullet in the shoulder which fractured the bone. No attempt was made to follow him up, and thirty-six hours later, his shoulder covered with a swarm of flies, he limped through the compound of the Inspection Bungalow, crossed a bridge flanked on the far side by a double row of tenanted houses, the occupants of which stood at their doors to watch him pass, entered the gate of a walled-in compound and took possession of a vacant godown. Twenty-four hours later, possibly alarmed by the number of people who had collected from neighbouring villages to see him, he left the compound the way he had entered it, passed our gate, and made his way to the lower end of our village. A bullock belonging to one of our tenants had died the previous night and had been dragged into some bushes at the edge of the village; this the tiger found, and here he remained a few days, quenching his thirst at an irrigation furrow.

When we came down from the hills two months later, the tiger was living on small animals (calves, sheep, goats, etc.) that he was able to catch on the outskirts of the village. By March his wound had healed, leaving his right foot turned inwards. Returning to the forest where he had been wounded, he levied heavy toll on the village cattle, taking, for safety's sake, but one meal off each and in this way killing five times as many as he would ordinarily have done. The zamindar who had wounded him and who had a herd of some four hundred head of cows and buffaloes was the chief sufferer.

In the succeeding years he gained as much in size as in reputation, and many were the attempts made by sportsmen, and others, to bag him.

One November evening, a villager, armed with a single-barrel muzzle loading gun, set out to try to bag a pig, selecting for his ground machan an isolated bush growing in a twenty-yard-wide rowkah (dry watercourse) running down the centre of some broken ground. This ground was rectangular, flanked on the long sides by cultivated land and on the short sides by a road, and by a ten-foot canal that formed the boundary between our cultivation and the forest. In front of the man was a four-foot-high bank with a cattle track running along the upper edge; behind him a patch of dense scrub. At 8 p.m. an animal appeared on the track and, taking what aim he could, he fired. On receiving the shot the animal fell off the bank, and passed within a few feet of the man, grunting as it entered the scrub behind. Casting aside his blanket, the man ran to his hut two hundred yards away. Neighbours soon collected and, on hearing the man's account, came to the conclusion that a pig had been hard hit. It would be a pity, they said, to leave the pig for hyenas and jackals to eat, so a lantern was lit and as a party of six bold spirits set out to retrieve the bag, one of my tenants (who declined to join the expedition, and who confessed to me later that he had no stomach for looking for wounded pig in dense scrub in the dark) suggested that the gun should be loaded and taken.

His suggestion was accepted and, as a liberal charge of powder was being rammed home, the wooden ramrod jammed and broke inside the barrel. A trivial accident which undoubtedly saved the lives of six men. The broken rod was eventually and after great trouble extracted, the gun loaded, and the party set off.

Arrived at the spot where the animal had entered the bushes, a careful search was made and, on blood being found, every effort to find the 'pig' was made; it was not until the whole area had been combed out that the quest for that night was finally abandoned. Early next morning the search was resumed, with the addition of my informant of weak stomach, who was a better woodsman than his companions and who, examining the ground under a bush where there was a lot of blood, collected and brought some blood-stained hairs to me which I recognized as tiger's hairs. A brother sportsman was with me for the day and together we went to have a look at the ground.

The reconstruction of jungle events from signs on the ground has always held great interest for me. True, one's deductions are sometimes wrong, but they are also sometimes right. In the present instance I was right in placing the wound in the inner forearm of the right foreleg, but was wrong in assuming the leg had been broken and that the tiger was a young animal and a stranger to the locality.

There was no blood beyond the point where the hairs had been found and, as tracking on the hard ground was impossible, I crossed the canal to where the cattle track ran through a bed of sand. Here from the pugmarks I found that the wounded animal was not a young tiger as I had assumed, but my old friend the Pipal Pani tiger who, when taking a shortcut through the village, had in the dark been mistaken for a pig.

Once before when badly wounded he had passed through the settlement without harming man or beast, but he was older now, and if driven by pain and hunger might do considerable damage. A disconcerting prospect, for the locality was thickly populated, and I was due to leave within the week, to keep an engagement that could not be put off.

For three days I searched every bit of the jungle between the canal and the foothills, an area of about four square miles, without finding any trace of the tiger. On the fourth afternoon, as I was setting out to continue the search, I met an old woman and her son hurriedly leaving the jungle. From them I learnt that the tiger was calling near the foothills and that all the cattle in the jungle had stampeded. When out with a rifle I invariably go alone; it is safer in a mix-up, and one can get through the jungle more silently. However, I stretched a point on this occasion, and let the boy accompany me since he was very keen on showing me where he had heard the tiger.

Arrived at the foothills, the boy pointed to a dense bit of cover, bounded on the far side by the fire-track to which I have already referred, and on the near side by the Pipal Pani stream. Running parallel to and about a hundred yards from the stream was a shallow depression some twenty feet wide, more or less open on my side and fringed with bushes on the side nearer the stream. A well-used path crossed the depression at right angles. Twenty yards from the path, and on the open side of the depression, was a small tree. If the tiger came down the path he would in all likelihood stand for a shot on clearing the bushes. Here I decided to take my stand and, putting the boy into the tree with his feet on a level with my head and instructing him to signal with his toes if from his raised position he saw the tiger before I did, I put my back to the tree and called.

You, who have spent as many years in the jungle as I have, need no description of the call of a tigress in search of a mate, and to you less fortunate ones I can only say that the call, to acquire which necessitates close observation and the liberal use of throat salve, cannot be described in words.

To my great relief, for I had crawled through the jungle for three days with finger on trigger, I was immediately answered from a distance of about five hundred yards, and for half an hour thereafter—it may have been less and certainly appeared more—the call was tossed back and forth. On the one side the urgent summons of the king, and on the other, the subdued and coaxing answer of his handmaiden. Twice the boy signalled, but I had as yet seen nothing of the tiger, and it was not until the setting sun was flooding the forest with golden light that he suddenly appeared, coming down the path at a fast walk with never a pause as he cleared the bushes. When halfway across the depression, and just as I was raising the rifle, he turned to the right and came straight towards me.

This manoeuvre, unforeseen when selecting my stand, brought him nearer than I had intended he should come and, moreover, presented me with a head shot which at that short range I was not prepared to take. Resorting to an old device, learned long years ago and successfully used on similar occasions, the tiger was brought to a stand without being alarmed. With one paw poised, he slowly raised his head, exposing as he did so his chest and throat. After the impact of the heavy bullet, he struggled to his feet and tore blindly through the forest, coming down with a crash within a few yards of where, attracted by the calling of a chital hind one November morning, I had first seen his pugmarks.

It was only then that I found he had been shot under a misapprehension, for the wound which I feared might make him dangerous proved on examination to be almost healed and caused by a pellet of lead having severed a small vein in his right forearm.

Pleasure at having secured a magnificent trophy—he measured 10' 3" over curves and his winter coat was in perfect condition—was not unmixed with regret, for never again would the jungle folk and I listen with held breath to his deep-throated call resounding through the foothills, and never again would his familiar pugmarks show on the game paths that he and I had trodden for fifteen years.

The Tyger

WILLIAM BLAKE

Tyger tyger, burning bright,
In the forests of the night;
What immortal hand or eye,
Could frame thy fearful symmetry?

In what distant deeps or skies.
Burnt the fire of thine eyes?
On what wings dare he aspire?
What the hand, dare seize the fire?

And what shoulder, & what art,
Could twist the sinews of thy heart?
And when thy heart began to beat,
What dread hand? & what dread feet?

What the hammer? what the chain,
In what furnace was thy brain?

What the anvil? what dread grasp.
Dare its deadly terrors clasp!

When the stars threw down their spears
And water'd heaven with their tears:
Did he smile his work to see?
Did he who made the Lamb make thee?

Tyger tyger burning bright,
In the forests of the night:
What immortal hand or eye,
Dare frame thy fearful symmetry?

The Hungry Tiger of Oz

RUTH PLUMLY THOMPSON

It was the Cowardly Lion who had coaxed the Hungry Tiger to the capitol. The Cowardly Lion, himself, had come there with Dorothy and the Scarecrow and grown so fond of the place and its people that he had returned to the jungle for his old friend, the Hungry Tiger. And like the Cowardly Lion, the Hungry Tiger had never been able to tear himself away from this dear and delightful city. Indeed life without the love of Dorothy, Betsy and Trot, the trust and affection of little Ozma, and the companionship of all the merry dwellers in the castle, would not be worth a soup bone. So the Hungry Tiger had never gone back, but at times the longing for real tiger food almost overcame him.

‘I wonder if stuffing would help,’ sighed the poor beast, licking his chops hungrily. ‘I wonder—’

‘What?’ wheezed an oily voice, almost in his ear. The Hungry Tiger, supposing himself to be alone, had spoken aloud, and springing up found himself face to face with an ugly, red-faced and exceedingly disagreeable-looking stranger. He was dressed in robes of pink, gold embroidered slippers and a simply enormous turban, that wagged from side to side as he talked. An oddly twisted cane swung from his left wrist and as he extended his hand in greeting, the Hungry Tiger jumped back in alarm, for the stranger’s thumb was blazing away merrily. It was Ippty, Chief Scribe of Rash, for the hurry-cane had brought him straight to the royal gardens of the Emerald City of Oz.

‘Am I addressing the Hungry Tiger of Oz?’ inquired Ippty. ‘And are you still hungry?’ he asked eagerly.

‘What if I am?’ growled the Hungry Tiger, blinking suspiciously at Irasha’s singular messenger. ‘What if I am?’

'Come with me,' said Ippty, mysteriously. 'Come with me, famous and famished member of the feline family, and you will never know hunger more!'

'Who are you?' rumbled the Hungry Tiger, sitting up and beginning to pant a little from astonishment. 'Who are you and what are you doing here?'

'I am Ippty, Chief Scribe of Irasha the Rough, and I am here to offer you an important position at the Court of Rash. Come to Rash,' begged Ippty, glancing uneasily over his shoulder, for he was not anxious to meet any of the Oz celebrities. 'Come, before we are discovered!'

'Rash!' coughed the Hungry Tiger impatiently. 'Why should I go to that measly little Kingdom when I am perfectly happy and contented here?'

'Because!' Bending over and splattering the Hungry Tiger with hot candle grease from his thumb, Ippty began whispering earnestly in his ear. At first, the Hungry Tiger's tail lashed and twirled with fury, but as Ippty continued, he grew calmer, and a queer longing crept into his great yellow eyes.

'Stand back fellow,' he mumbled crossly, 'you will singe off my whiskers, and kindly remove your pencil from my eye.'

'But you will come?' Straightening up, Ippty put his bristly hand behind him and regarded the Hungry Tiger expectantly. 'Not less than one prisoner a day, sometimes as many as ten,' he repeated persuasively.

'Humph!' grunted the tiger, half closing his eyes. Already Ippty's wicked plan was beginning to tempt him. Surely eating criminals would not be wrong, or at least, not so very wrong.

'And these prisoners are dangerous fellows, I suppose?' he asked casually, trying to appear careless and unconcerned about the whole queer business.

'Villains, thieves and robbers, rascally fat rogues who are a menace to the country. By eating them you will be doing Rash a real service,' Ippty assured him.

'And where is Rash?' asked the Hungry Tiger, waving his tail inquiringly.

'In the southwestern corner of Ev,' answered the Scribe, with a wave that nearly put out his thumb. 'And if you are ready, dear beast, we will start at once.'

'Ev!' spluttered the tiger, 'Why that's miles away. I was there long ago, when Ozma, Dorothy and Billina rescued Prince Evardo from the Gnome King. Too far!' yawned the Hungry Tiger, rolling over on the dewy grass. 'I'm too tired for such a journey.'

'No trip at all!' Ippty touched the hurry-cane and in a few words explained its curious mechanism, following it up with such a tempting description of the Rash prisoners that the Hungry Tiger's appetite got the better of his conscience.

'I'll go,' he agreed gruffly, 'but only for a few days, remember.' Ippty said nothing, but smiled wickedly to himself. Then, stuffing the directions for their return into the hurry-cane, he sprang upon the Hungry Tiger's back. Next instant, in a flash of fire and smoke, they had disappeared from the garden.

'What was that?' gasped Dorothy, clutching Ozma by the sleeve. Both little girls, crouched behind a button bush, had seen the strange flash.

'Lightning, I guess!' shuddered Ozma. 'Let's run back to the castle, Dorothy. A thunder storm's coming!'

The Hungry Tiger in Rash

It was night time when Ippty and the Hungry Tiger arrived at the pink palace. Travelling by hurry-cane is a hair-raising experience, let me tell you. Showing the breathless beast to a luxurious apartment, the Chief Scribe hurried off to the Pasha, and until long after midnight the two whispered and conferred together. Of course it was about the Hungry Tiger that they talked.

'A saucy, but serviceable brute,' finished Ippty, blowing out his thumb, 'and he will require watching, Your Highness, for would not a tiger fed on criminals grow dangerous?'

'We'll lock him up in the prison courtyard,' declared Irashi, rubbing his hands gleefully together, 'then there'll be no chance of his running away or chewing off our heads. Good work, old Butter-tub, I'll raise your wages for this.' And clapping his Chief Scribe on the back, Irashi tumbled into bed and was soon snoring loudly.

The Hungry Tiger did not find falling asleep so easy. Already he regretted his rash action in coming with Ippty. Padding up and down the big bedroom, he began anxiously to reflect upon the duties of his new office. Was it right or wrong to eat the Rash criminals? What would Ozma think if she knew? The gentle face of the little fairy kept rising reproachfully between him and the thought of the fat and tempting prisoners. 'I'll stay just a few days,' groaned the poor tiger at last, trying to put Ozma out of his mind, 'and only eat the very worst and wickedest ones. I hope they'll not taste too bad,' he yawned, sinking down wearily on the soft pink rug, 'nor have too many knives and swords in their pockets. Hah, hoh, hum!' With a great yawn, the tired tiger rolled over and fell into a troubled sleep.

A shrill blast of trumpets wakened him next morning and a few moments later Ippty came to conduct him to the Pasha. Irashi had craftily arranged to receive the Hungry Tiger in the prison courtyard, and surrounded by the Rash Guardsmen, with Fizzenpop standing anxiously at his side, he waited for the tiger to appear. The walk from the palace to the prison was not long, but it gave the Hungry Tiger quite a glimpse of the country and the people. The palace and all of the cottages and stores were of pink stone. Pink trees lined the pink marble walks and even the sky had a rosy glow. The Rashers, themselves, hurrying to and fro in their tremendous flapping turbans, oddly quilted robes and soft pink slippers, seemed pleasant enough fellows and again the Hungry Tiger's conscience began to trouble him. But it was too late to turn back now, so he stalked uncomfortably after Ippty. The prison itself looked quite like a wing of the pink palace and unsuspectingly the Hungry Tiger passed through the great golden gates and into a high walled court.

'Ah hah!' exclaimed Irashi, as he advanced majestically to the centre of the courtyard. 'So here he is at last, the famous and famished tiger of Oz. And in uniform, too. Is it not splendid that the future jailer of Rash should wear stripes,' chuckled the Pasha, poking Fizzenpop playfully in the ribs. 'Even now our prisoners will go behind the bars—after they are eaten,' he whispered hoarsely, fearing Fizzenpop might not get the joke. Ippty burst into a loud roar, but the Grand Vizier, after one look at the huge figure of the tiger, began to tremble from top to toe. The Hungry Tiger, himself, was not at all pleased with his reception.

'Are you laughing at me?' he growled, lashing his tail and showing so many teeth the Rash Guardsmen took to their pink heels. 'Are you laughing at ME?'

'No! No, certainly not,' grunted Irashi, moving hurriedly toward the gates. 'I hope you will be most comfortable and happy here.' At each word, Irashi took a great leap, followed closely by Ippty and Fizzenpop. By the time he finished his sentence and before the Hungry Tiger realized what was happening, all three were on the other side of the gates and the tiger, himself, was locked fast in the courtyard.

'Stay there, you saucy monster,' puffed Irashi, shaking his sceptre playfully, and taking

Fizzenpop by one arm and Ippty by the other, he waddled off, leaving the Hungry Tiger to reflect upon his folly. First he hurled himself again and again at the golden gates, then he ran round and round the prison yard examining every inch of the high walls. But it was useless. There was not so much as a chink in the marble blocks. Raging with anger at Irashi and disgusted with himself for being so easily caught, he crouched down in a gloomy corner of the yard to think. All choice in the matter of eating the Rash prisoners was now removed, for, as he sadly reflected, there would probably be nothing else to eat. But eating prisoners, when you are free and happy, and eating prisoners because there is nothing else are entirely different matters and already half the pleasure was gone from the experiment. How was he to escape from this miserable little monarch? Would Dorothy and Betsy miss him? Why, oh why, had he not listened to the voice of his conscience or even had himself stuffed, as the Wizard suggested?

Blinking his eyes mournfully, the Hungry Tiger began to feel sorry not only for the Rash prisoners, but dreadfully sorry for himself, for was he not a prisoner, too? He had plenty of time to feel sorry, for not a soul came near him all day—not even a Rash mouse. There was a tub of water in the corner of the yard, but nothing to eat, and as the shadows grew longer and longer the poor tiger grew hungrier and hungrier. Betsy's party seemed years ago and when, towards evening, shrill screams from the wall announced the approach of Irashi and the guards, he looked up almost hopefully to see whether they were bringing a prisoner. They were. Propped up between two guards, and advancing most unwillingly, was a tall turbaned figure.

'Here!' shouted Irashi, leaning far over the wall, 'Here is your supper. Eat this rogue at once. He has wakened me from my sacred nap with his horrible howling.'

'I suppose I'll have to,' mumbled the Hungry Tiger uncomfortably to himself, and growling to keep his courage up and his conscience down, he advanced towards the wall just as the guardsmen dropped the luckless Rasher over.

He landed lightly on the balls of his feet and after one look at the Hungry Tiger pulled his turban over his eyes and began to screech with terror.

'Eat him up! Shut him up! What's the matter, have you no teeth?' bawled Irashi covering his ears.

'I never dine till ten o'clock,' answered the Hungry Tiger stiffly. He was not going to be bullied by the wretched little sovereign of Rash. 'And I never eat until I am alone,' he growled raising his roar above the wails of the prisoner.

'Suit yourself,' grumbled Irashi. But secretly he was disappointed. To watch the Hungry Tiger devour the prisoner would have been a real treat for the wicked little Pasha. Covering both ears to drown the poor fellow's doleful yells, he scrambled down the steps on the other side of the wall. 'We'll return later to see if he is eaten,' puffed the little Pasha, turning back towards the castle, and the guardsmen, exchanging uneasy glances, clanked after him. As soon as they were alone, the Hungry Tiger approached the prisoner.

'Would you mind stopping that noise?' he begged earnestly. 'You're really spoiling my supper.'

'Your supper?' gulped the Rasher, trembling violently. 'Do you expect me to submit to eating without a sound?'

'Well, I wish that you would,' sighed the tiger hopefully. 'I never cared for music with my meals. Now don't be frightened, I won't hurt you—much. If you were not so tall, I'd swallow you whole.'

'Oh!' groaned the prisoner falling upon his knees, 'Have you no heart? No conscience? Are you really cruel enough to devour a poor fellow like me?' At each word, the Hungry Tiger recoiled a bit further.

'But what can I do? I've nothing else to eat and it is the Rash law that you should perish. By the way, what was your crime?' he asked sadly. Now that the time for eating a live man was at hand, he found himself curiously disturbed.

'I'm a singer,' began the prisoner, in a choked and frightened voice. 'This afternoon, hoping to earn a few Rash pence, I stopped beneath the palace balcony and—' Straightening up and throwing out his chest, the singer burst into tears and song, mingling them so thoroughly the Hungry Tiger was soon crying like a baby himself. Without the tears, the song went something like this:

'Oh why must lovely roses die?
Oh why, snif! snif! Oh why, say why?
Oh why must hay be cut and mown
In its first hey-day? Groan, snif, groan!
And why must grass be trodden down
And trees cut up to build a town?
Should little lambs grow into chops
And hang around in butcher shops?
No! No! I weep, it is too sad.
Snif, snuffle, snif, I feel so sad!'

'So do I!' roared the Hungry Tiger. 'Stop! Stop! I am positively ill. What's that?' That was a large bunch of bananas. It came whistling over the wall, followed by three onions, a sausage, a squash pie and a head of cabbage.

'They always throw things when I sing,' sobbed the singer, drying his eyes on his pink sleeve.

'Pass me that sausage,' gulped the Hungry Tiger in a faint voice.

'Are—are'nt you going to eat me?' stuttered the sad singer, offering the sausage fearfully and jumping back as if he expected the tiger to snap off his arm. Between bites, and the sausage took only two, the Hungry Tiger shook his head.

'Not now,' he answered wearily. 'I might have swallowed *you*, but that song! Never! A man full of music like that would ruin my digestion. How's the pie?'

'Squashed,' said the singer, in a depressed whisper. 'Try the onions.' He held them out hopefully, but the Hungry Tiger only shuddered.

'Eat them yourself,' he advised gloomily, 'you seem to enjoy crying.' Reaching for a banana, the Hungry Tiger ripped off the skin and swallowed it whole. Three more, he treated in the same reckless fashion. Then licking his whiskers, he regarded the sad singer reproachfully. 'You may go now,' he said gruffly. 'Your singing is outrageous, but you are neither wicked enough to satisfy my conscience nor fat enough to satisfy my appetite. Go—go—before—'

'But how can I go,' moaned the singer, waving despairingly at the high walls. I do not know whether his tears were from grief, gratitude or onions. (He had eaten all three by this time.)

'Well, you can't stay here,' rumbled the tiger anxiously, 'for you're supposed to be eaten.'

'I'll hide,' muttered the prisoner, glaring around wildly. But there was no place in the whole pink yard where he could conceal himself. Round and round tore the worried Rasher and round and round after him nosed the Hungry Tiger and, just as the moon rose up over the pink turrets of the palace, they discovered a loose block in the stone pavings. Scratching frantically with his powerful claws the Hungry Tiger managed to dig up the whole block and dragging it aside found a small damp underground chamber.

The sad singer was overjoyed, when he peeped into the dark hole, for he had become very nervous, in his fear that the tiger would soon decide to eat him. To tell the truth, the Hungry Tiger was glad himself. The sad singer did not look very good to eat.

'There!' grunted the Hungry Tiger, thrusting the singer in and throwing some bananas and a head of cabbage after him. 'Be quiet and whatever you do, *don't sing*!' He had just pushed the block back, leaving a small crevice to give the prisoner air, when Irashi and Ippty appeared upon the wall.

'Ah! He has eaten him!' cried Irashi rapturously, and clapping his hands like a child, he began to address the Hungry Tiger in most affectionate terms, promising him a dozen prisoners upon the morrow. But the Hungry Tiger merely turned his back and gazed solemnly up at the moon, and seeing nothing was to be got out of him, Irashi and his wicked scribe tip-toed off to bed, well pleased with the new jailer of Rash. The Hungry Tiger himself, in spite of a horribly hollow feeling (what is a sausage and four bananas to a tiger?) soon fell asleep. And perhaps because he had done nothing to trouble his kind old conscience, he dreamed that he was safely back in the Emerald City with dear little Ozma of Oz.

The Tiger Whisperer

ANJANA BASU

Rohan's Dadubhai had some business in Jagdalpur over the Dusserah weekend so he decided to take Rohan along with him. Rohan had never seen anything like the Jagdalpur Maidan.

It was filled with people from the nearby villages carrying their kuldevatas or angdeos on bamboo poles accompanied by their shamans. The whole Maidan had become a shaking, quaking celebration filled with deities on poles, music and entranced shamans. Rohan was particularly fascinated by the shamans. 'They're head banging,' he told his Dadubhai. 'Why do they do that?'

'The music makes them jerk their heads like that,' his Dadubhai said. 'Each of their angdeos has their own special mantra.'

'And who do they worship?' Rohan asked, looking at the poles with their tinsel draping and carvings.

'The gods of the forest. Deer, tigers...'

'Tigers?' Rohan asked, pricking up his ears.

His grandfather smiled. 'They can talk to the animals here sometimes,' he said. 'Especially to tigers.'

At that moment the musicians playing the music for the angdeos became louder and nothing could be heard except the sound of the pipes. The Maharajah of Jagdalpur arrived and was greeted in a rush of gods and shamans. 'Time to go back,' Dadubhai told Rohan. 'And all this dust isn't good for either of us.'

That night, sitting on the veranda of their cottage and listening to the howl of jackals in the distance, his grandfather told Rohan the story of Kalibhit Bhomka. 'What's a bhomka?' Rohan wanted to know.

'A bhomka is a tiger whisperer—you would call him a shaman perhaps.'

'They bang heads with tigers?'

Rohan's grandfather shook his head and sipped his cup of steaming tea. The evening was cool and it felt as if winter was round the corner. 'The bhomka actually does duty as the head priest of Baghdeo. He is supposed to make sure that tigers do not disturb the villagers and whenever a tiger appears around a village, he says special prayers to Baghdeo.

'Kalibhit Bhomka was known for the strength of his prayers. Every time he needed to do a yajna to Baghdeo, it was inevitably successful. The villagers gave him whatever he asked for to complete the yajna, whether it was goats or cows or ghee, and Kalibhit's protection never failed. At the climax of the yajna, Kalibhit would offer a large iron nail to Baghdeo, sprinkle it with holy water and place it in the heart of the sacred fire. When the fire burned down to glowing embers, he would pull the nail out of the coals and take it from the temple to the forest. Just inside the fringe of trees was a huge sal tree with a hollow that looked like the toothless mouth of an old man. Kalibhit would hammer that nail into the bark of the tree uttering loud mantras as he did so. Shortly after the nail was gleaming in the tree, a tiger would appear from the bushes and drag his claws across the nail.

'It was like a signature,' Dadubhai said, 'the tiger had accepted the terms and conditions laid down by Baghdeo and promised not to harm the villagers.'

'Well tigers sharpen their claws on trees anyway,' Rohan pointed out.

'I'm sure Kalibhit knew that, but he was a shaman and shamans do things differently. There used to be shamans in other parts of Madhya Pradesh who would drag tigers out of the bushes by their ears and whisper mantras to them while the villagers who were lucky enough to see it would hold their breath in awe. Or they used to scatter all kinds of charms on the roads leading to the village, like little wooden beds and household furniture...'

A jackal howled and Rohan looked out at the dark patch of lawn outside. He couldn't see anything because there were lights from the walkways dotting the area. 'They won't come near the building,' his grandfather said consolingly. 'Probably hanging around the kitchen hoping for scraps.' Rohan's eyes still scanned the darkness some more. Then he turned back to his grandfather and said, 'What about Kalibhit?'

There were shamans, his grandfather told him, who claimed to know strange roots that they would burn and then bury in the earth. The scent was enough to keep tigers away. Kalibhit however had no such gimmicks. He lived by his mantras and the huge sal tree with all the nails in the bark. The tree which had a toothless old man's mouth hollow was scarred by claw marks.

Kalibhit had no family. Perhaps no village girl would have been able to live with his fearsome power. Certainly to have tigers stalking around would have needed a bravehearted girl, someone like Ma Durga herself. Girls like those were few and far between though some of them had been known to tackle tigers with their sickles while out cutting grass. An old woman cooked for him and her granddaughter came to clean his hut and sweep the courtyard with sal twigs. He spent his days deep in mantras or reading the clouds and the wind.

One morning, when he had gone to the well to collect water, he noticed a huge pugmark imprinted in the wet soil just where he might be expected to notice it. Kalibhit walked past the pugmark without turning a hair, filled his earthen pot and returned to his hut. There he found a group of men waiting for him.

'Bhomka, a new tiger has come to Hoshanbad.'

'His tracks are all round the fields. They are this big!' They spread their hands indicating the size. Kalibhit knew it was a big tiger but he let the villagers talk. He wanted to know what he would get for doing the yajna because there was no bhomka like him for twenty villages.

'Perhaps,' Dadubhai said slowly, 'Kalibhit had become a little arrogant but then he had been practising his art for years. He had no one to train after him, unless he talked to the young girl who swept his courtyard. And somehow training a girl went against everything that he stood for. He listened to the villagers making their promises and finally agreed that he would summon Baghdeo with all the power in his control.

'There was a great sweeping and swishing around the Baghdeo temple. The young girl was seen carrying in armfuls of brush and twigs. Smoke billowed from her grandmother's cook pots.'

'What was she cooking?' Rohan asked.

Dadubhai shrugged, 'No one knew. They could have asked the girl, but they didn't dare. Many swore that it smelt unearthly. But then, they would have sworn anything.

'Finally, the yajna was ready. Kalibhit wrapped his tiger skin dhoti and put a long red tilak on his forehead, then made his stately way into the cave-like temple. The girl who was watching him, as she always did, wondered whether he had noticed that the clusters of white clouds in the sky looked oddly like tiger's pugmarks. At any other time, she would have pointed it out to him but when he was dressed for an encounter with Baghdeo, no one was allowed to speak a single word. The only sounds would be sounds of mantras and the clashing of bells. The villagers came to stand with the girl. It was a long yajna and the prayers were filled with power. Finally Kalibhit appeared at the entrance with the nail shining in his fingers and a copper hammer in one hand.

'Slowly he made his way to the forest to the tree with the old man's hollow. The track that he followed had a pugmark beside it and that caught his eye. But then the yajna was supposed to summon the tiger for the signing of the contract. The villagers heard the tap tap of the hammer as the nail was driven into the bark. "When will the tiger come?" they asked the girl.

'"Soon enough," she answered. "Look, here comes the Bhomka."

'Kalibhit came out of the trees with a strange glow on his face. He looked at the villagers and said, "Baghdeo has sent him." Almost immediately the trees rustled and there was a growl from behind the Bhomka.

'It was the custom to go the next day to check whether the tiger had drawn his claws across the nail. To go the same day would have been foolhardy—dusk was falling and the cattle were being driven home. They would all go the next morning led by Kalibhit in a triumphant procession and Kalibhit would be given new dhotis, ghee, wheat, mahua fruit, mangoes and sackfuls of rice as his reward. Everyone in the village contributed from their fields.

'The sun sank in a ball of red. Dusk fell over the village and the cows returned in a haze of dust. Fires were lit as the evening meals were cooked and the village went about settling down for the night. Just when the dinners had been eaten, everything was quiet and the mothers had rocked their children to sleep, there was the sudden shriek of a night bird followed by a tremendous roaring that filled the darkness with thunder. Everyone sat up in their beds and the men began fumbling for their sickles and knives.

'However, there were no bleats from the cattle and goats in their thorn barricades, so the village began to relax again. The young girl in her grandmother's hut heard it too. She clutched the covers closer and did not move. She knew Baghdeo's call when she heard it.

'The next morning the villager elders, sickles in hand made their way to the gnarled old sal tree. Kalibhit was not there, but there were claw marks across the nail and fresh pugmarks at the base of the tree. The contract had been signed and Kalibhit's reward had to be delivered to his hut. Shouldering sacks and bags the women and children made their way to Kalibhit's compound. They were chattering, pushing, shoving and certain that they would be safe from tigers for another year—quite forgetting the disturbance in the night. The door to Kalibhit's hut was open and the girl was sweeping the compound. She hadn't seen him, she said, he must have gone to get water from the well. He did it quite often, leaving the door open for her. Or perhaps he had gone to the tree to check the tiger's signature.

'No, they said, they hadn't seen him there, but the tiger had most certainly signed, clawed the nail so hard that the surface was scratched. The girl frowned and put down her broom. She made her way to the well followed by the women and children.

'The first thing they saw was Kalibhit's pot lying shattered on the ground. There was a pugmark in the wet earth. Something had been dragged away from the water and the drag marks were in the direction of Baghdeo's temple.

'Kalibhit's tiger skin was lying in front of the temple. It had been clawed into shreds. There was a trail of blood that led away towards the forest—blood that was still moist and therefore fresh. The women clutched their children in horror. The girl took a deep breath and walked into the temple. Barring the flickering lamp in front of the tiger god, the place was empty.

'When she came out she found the village elders waiting in front of the cave. Her eyes lowered to the ground, she mumbled, "He is not there. We must look in the forest." She could feel the alarm coming from the crowd. Something like this had not happened in more years than anyone could remember and where was Kalibhit? How had his powerful yajna failed? They fidgeted, unwilling to follow that blood trail into the forest.

'The girl said, "I shall go." And she began walking. Slowly she could hear the shuffle of feet start up behind her. But after a while as they neared the sal tree the blood trail disappeared. All that remained was the pugmark they had seen at the base of the tree. Barring the twittering of birds, the forest was still. There were no warning tiger sounds from barking deer or monkeys.

'"I will look for him," the girl announced and none of the elders challenged her.'

'How did she get so brave?' Rohan wanted to know.

'Perhaps she had learnt a lot of things from Kalibhit while sweeping his courtyard,' his Dadubhai answered. 'Who knows? For three days the girl was missing and her grandmother wailed that the evil tiger had taken her too. But, on the evening of the third day, as the cows were coming home, she appeared in the evening haze, an almost ghostly figure.

'"I did not find him," she said, when the village leaders came up to her. But she would not tell them where she had been.

'She and her grandmother moved into Kalibhit's hut and no one challenged her. One day she was found sitting by the well and modelling a tiger out of red earth. Into it she put the fragments of Kalibhit's broken pot. "This is for his funeral pyre," she answered, when people asked her. It was obvious to her that body or no body Kalibhit had to have a proper funeral.

'In three days no tiger had made its presence felt and there was the troubling feeling that if Kalibhit had a funeral it might just arouse that treacherous tiger that had killed him to rage against the village. If the girl heard the whispers she showed no sign. Her earth tiger sat on the edge of the well studded with shards of pottery and no one dared touch it. She swept the courtyard in front of the hut and lit the lamps in Baghdeo's temple.

'One morning, after lighting the lamps, she came out of the temple with a diya in her hand. She took the diya to the sal tree and ran the flame over that last fateful nail, burning away the tiger's claw marks. "What are you doing?" the village head asked her.

'"There is no point to this signature," answered the girl. "The tiger has broken its word." The villagers would have challenged the girl but they didn't—no one knew of any bhomkas within miles and no one dared to brave the forests to go looking for them. The girl burnt the bark and took the lamp back to the temple. There it flickered in front of Baghdeo and continued to flicker well into the darkness.

'When the temple mouth was dark, some people said that they heard a roar—but it may just have been thunder rumbling in the distant hills.

'Soon the girl began dragging wood into the clearing in front of the temple. Thick branches, brush, wood of all shapes and sizes, she got them all. Her hands were scratched and she had tied her hair into a thick rope so that it did not get in the way. She did not ask anyone to help her and no one offered. They stood and watched in between carrying out their daily chores. Once a man came running from the fields gasping that he had glimpsed the orange hide of a tiger but when the villagers reached there with their sickles there was no tiger to be seen. The girl ignored it all.

'Finally, exactly thirteen days after Kalibhit's disappearance and presumed death, the pyre was ready. "What are you going to put on that?" the village head asked the girl. The women had been busy trying to get some sort of answer from her grandmother but the old woman just shook her head, referred them to her granddaughter and returned to chopping vegetables. Life was easier for her in Kalibhit's hut though her granddaughter had insisted on returning the gifts of grain, and she did not intend to endanger that, praying that the village would not find another bhomka.

'In response to the village head, the girl fetched the earthen tiger that was still perched beside the well. She put it on the platform of branches and looked at it thoughtfully. Someone laughed and she whirled around as swiftly as a tiger, her eyes blazing. Beside the tiger she put a finely modelled pottery bedstead that she must have made in secret. Last of all, she dragged up the tattered blood-stained tiger skin. "I will light it at night," she told the assembled villagers, "when the moon is full."

'The rest of the day she spent in Baghdeo's temple with her grandmother grumbling that she had eaten nothing at all since she had starting building the pyre barring sips of milk.

'If she hadn't told them about the milk,' Dadubhai told Rohan, 'the villagers would have burnt her for being a witch. As it was, they were suspicious. No one had heard of a woman bhomka before, if that was what she was pretending to be.

'Everyone in the village was waiting for moonrise. And when the round moon finally lifted itself over the trees, exactly the same colour as a tiger's eye, the whole village was clustered around the pyre. Soon they saw a flame advancing in the darkness of the temple. It grew bigger and the girl who was carrying it appeared at the temple's entrance. She was draped in white with the rope of her hair over one shoulder. There was no tikka on her forehead. She carried the unwavering flame through the still night to the pyre and touched it to the brush and twigs at its base. The flame caught and leaped higher and higher. Smoke billowed and the moon was almost blotted out—or was it thick clouds which came from nowhere to veil the moon?

'The girl was chanting something, circling the pyre. The villagers could see her in between the smoke and the leaping tongues of flame. Sparks leapt out of the crackling heart of the pyre and scattered on the grass. Smaller tongues of flame danced wherever the grass caught. The fire had reached the tiger skin and there was the smell of burning hide and hair.

'And then came what some of them claimed they had half expected—a tremendous roar. An enormous tiger leaped out of the billowing smoke and flames towards the girl. She stood her ground. As the tiger pounced, she seemed to punch it in the eye. The smoke gusted in dense black clouds so one was too sure but some said the tiger collapsed and from its skin stood a gigantic Kalibhit roaring with rage, the silver nail in the girl's hand pointed at him and shining through the smoke and blackness. All the darkness and light seemed to collect at that sharp silver point and vanish into it.

'Then the night was clear, the pyre a blackened ruin and the moon's silver disk shone again.

'The next morning, as dawn was touching the sky with its golden fingers, the girl made her way to the forest. There she found the broken ruin of the sal tree, the open old man's toothless hollow gaping up at the sky.'

'So what was it all about?' Rohan wanted to know. The story had taken a long time and it was well past his bedtime. 'Was the tiger actually Kalibhit?'

'It's an old story,' his Dadubhai said, 'and no one really knows. Perhaps he was a tiger which is why he was able to make all those contracts with tigers. But you could say the whole story was really about what you call girl power. Anyway, time for you to go to bed. It's late.'

The Art of Hunting

DHAN GOPAL MUKHERJI

The ceremony of my initiation had a strange effect upon me. It burnt into my soul that no matter what vocation we choose, it should be considered as a responsibility and not as a holiday. I asked other boys who were initiated into other crafts, and they bore me out in my conclusion. A weaver lad who was initiated a month before me said: 'I know now that weaving is not only a vocation but also an adoration of God. I try to make beautiful fabrics to proclaim that I have not scamped my work, nor tried to hoodwink the Invisible.'

A carpenter six months after his initiation answered my questions as follows, 'I am glad I was put through the ceremony of initiation. I was imposed upon by its solemnity to swear not only to the others present but to myself that I would make beauty and utility for man. I am not afraid to be poor: if my hands are strong and my home free of famine, why should I fret for more riches.'

Our Hindu initiation gives courage to the young to live without the fear of poverty. Alas! I had no sister, so I cannot tell you of a young woman's initiation. I witnessed no such event. Now that India is becoming modernized and the time-tested ancient ceremony of initiation is slowly going out of fashion, it would be wise to record all its forms and names for the pleasure of posterity.

Later when I became a hunter by profession, my observation of animal life revealed to me that animals perform their own adoration of the sanctities, and also train and initiate their young.

Adoration of sunset and sunrise among birds and beasts is a common thing. In their eyes the light of the sun is the only God. So when he, the Lord of day arises, eagles wheel at the gates of the east like the ritual dancers in the temple of Nataraja; monkeys sit in silence on tree-tops, even squirrels interrupt their eternal quest for nuts and sit still on their branches till the hour of Light has passed. Sunset too they observe in similar fashion. Religion is necessary both for men and his younger brothers, the dumb souls whose speechlessness is more eloquent than man's speech.

Let me tell you now the tale of an animal's initiation. It was after I was thirty that one day I encountered a family of tigers. The parents were about six years old, and the younglings hardly four months. They were living in the Sunderbans—those beautiful woods of the deltas at the mouth of the Ganges. What a place, the Sunderbans! There the rivers are full of crocodiles and the ground savage with tigers, leopards, panthers and rhinoceros, not to mention wild buffaloes, vipers and tarantulas. The crocodiles were the most dangerous of these, I think, though troubles came from the large cats, and I was appointed by the State to find out why the tigers of the Sunderbans ate man.

I took up my abode in a village of about three score families on the bank of the Ganges. The river was tawny and so broad in those regions that you could hardly see the opposite shore. The village fronted the water as all Hindu settlements do, and behind us, beyond some cultivated land about two miles long and half a mile broad, lay the jungle. The jungle was about ten miles deep, separating us from the village on the other side of the delta. That human habitation was very large and had a weekly boat service to Calcutta about two hundred miles up the sacred river. This village was named Sundari, Beauty.

Our village had the magnificent name of Tajjabpore, Seat of Wonder. It was my duty to accompany the postman of Tajjabpore once a week across the jungle, going on a Tuesday and returning on a Thursday. It was during one of these trips, about the middle of June, that we came across Bagh, his wife Baghini, and their son and daughter. It was a very hot summer and the rain had not yet fallen in large quantities.

During the season of drought, animals, especially deer, elephant and wild buffaloes come near human habitation and assuage their hunger by eating up the growing grain fields. And since every animal follows its food, the big cats followed the vegetarians.

So one Tuesday morning as we crossed the grain fields and entered the woods, we came upon fourfold tiger pugs. Since it was nearly eight in the morning the postman and I concluded that all the tigers were fast asleep by now and it would do us no harm to go on their track. In another twenty minutes we came across a very dear place where the postman said that he saw something moving. We went forward to investigate, and came upon an amazing sight. There lay father and mother tiger on the bank of a small pond not far away. Since the rivers are full of crocodiles, in order to avoid trouble, wild animals generally drink from inland pools that never dry up. The sunlight fell profusely on the waters, and patches of it played on the plants and thorn bushes that framed them.

In order to find out what had happened to the two youngsters we climbed up a tree and looked down. We distinctly saw the raw skeleton of an animal lying between the parents, and before them about ten feet away, the two cubs were slowly approaching the water's edge to take a drink. It looked as if this was the first time they had gone to the water unaccompanied by Bagh and Baghini for they stepped gingerly: brother, who was the larger of the two, leading sister. They nosed about the shore until they came upon the tracks of the past, and no doubt inferred that since tigers had gone to the drinking place on that path before, the precedent must be adhered to.

First, brother stood over the water, looking about to make sure that no danger presented itself from any direction, then lowering his head—imitating the gestures of an old tiger—he took his drink. Next he turned round, making room for sister. She nosed his ear, as much as to say: 'Guard my rear while I drink.'

The boy did so with the gallantry of a young gentleman, then they slowly retraced their steps on their previous track to their parents. That display of caution—the sense that one should keep to the old and trusted paths—told me how sagacious young animals generally are.

Now that I had found them, I made up my mind to study as closely as possible the way tigers brought up their young, so I spent the following two months in tracking and watching them. It proved an easy task, for the little ones could not wander very far. The shortness of their legs permitted them no long hunting trips. Even though the monsoon had come and more rain had fallen, yet they stayed between the two villages that lay at either end of the jungle.

The way the parents taught the cubs to hunt was a superb lesson in education. Step by step they were taught. The day they killed their first large calf, I was with them. This was what happened. Towards the end of June it had rained steadily for a whole week. At the end of it when the sun shone again, the cattle of the village went to graze in the forest, for there, like steady green sparks from an anvil, the grass had suddenly shot up. But monsoon weather is freakish. About midday a swift thunderstorm frightened the cows and their herdsmen, and they sped home without waiting to count the heads of the cattle. That is why they did not round up a large calf who was left to find his way home all alone after the storm had passed.

I, who was on a tree during the rain, beheld him straggling along and eating all he could of the tender grass. Suddenly I saw two purple streaks run in the sunlight, and stop facing the poor calf. It was mother tiger and her son. Soon the wind blew the odour of their presence towards the lost creature. He whinneyed almost like a horse as he smelt tiger, and turning round dashed for the jungle. There in the shadows he saw father tiger and daughter. I shouted from the tree top—but too late. A flash of purple, yellow and black—the calf's tail raised stiff in the air—then....

That evening when I returned to Tajjabpore and told the villagers what had happened they scolded me for not saving that poor calf. It never entered their heads that had I come between their food and the four cats, I would not be there to tell the tale! I never shoot an animal, as a rule, except from great necessity, and on this particular afternoon, I had not taken my rifle with me, though as a forest warden of the State I was allowed a gun. I explained to the villagers that tigers, even the born man-eaters, do not kill their first human victim until he comes between them and their prey at a critical moment. But once the tiger has tasted human blood, and learns the helplessness of his prey, he does not hesitate to kill whenever he corners man. Moreover man is a biped: he cannot run away as fast as a deer or any other quadruped, and that makes any human being, without a rifle, helpless before the striped and spotted enemy.

After the killing of that large calf, the village was nervous, and set up special watches for its cattle. As for human beings, none ventured abroad after nightfall. I said, 'If a man carries a burning torch or a well-lit hurricane lantern, no beast of prey will go out of its way to meet him. The more you are seen at night, the wider berth they will give our village, but if you do not take the offensive, the animals will become aggressive. They smell fear more quickly than you know, and your fear will frighten them to attack you.' But only the postman agreed with me. It was the two of us out of that entire village who ever went abroad at any hour, day or night. Though I always carried a torch, I rarely lighted it. My eyes were extremely keen: in fact the keenest of all the hunters of my time. I could see in the dark better than antelopes. Sometimes I was credited with the eye power of the tiger, so at night, unless I wanted to keep the animals far away, I never carried a flaming torch. So now my eyes had to serve me to the utmost, for I was studying the two cubs and their education at all hours, and they led me into all kinds of places. At first, the parents, I noticed, did all the hunting, though the children stalked the prey and frightened them yet the cubs were not pushed to leap and kill. That final deed the parents shared between them. Watching the parents educated the children considerably, yet in spite of this, the parents took the children to places where it would be possible for them to leap and kill if they wished. One day I saw them do an interesting thing. It was around midday, near the drinking place. The parents and the children were lying wide awake near the pond. The wind was blowing from the opposite direction. Soon at the other end of the pond came a wild buffalo family. Father and mother stood on either side while the young steer, about two months old, drank his fill. Then the father took his drink while the other two watched. Last drank the cow, whose rear the bull and the calf protected. Then the parents lay down, their backs to the water, and before them in the jungle their child grazed and frisked about. From my tree-top I could see mother tiger pushing away her babies from her as if they were too big to be cuddled. So they trotted out, and soon caught the scent of the buffaloes. For awhile I lost sight of them, and then I saw them coming towards the guileless bull calf playing in the grass. Now quickly the cubs crouched and vanished again from sight, but they crawled nearer and nearer, as I could tell from the protruding of their snouts every few seconds from under leaves or saplings here and there. At last they attacked the young steer who mooed for help. Moo! ... Instantly like two black rocks the cow and the bull charged. Their bellowing filled the jungle with terror. The tiger cubs fled helter-skelter. Why the buffaloes waited so long ere they ran to the protection of their calf I could not make out, but probably they too were educating him as the tigers were educating their young. When the cubs reached home, they looked crestfallen. The daughter went to her father and the boy put his head under his mother's chin.

Another time the young male cub attacked a baby monkey. No sooner had he done so than the father and mother monkeys fell on him like two friends. They slapped his face so hard that he let go of the baby monkey whose tail his paws had held like a vise. No sooner had he released it than all three of them scurried up a tree and jabbered in terror. That set flocks and flocks of monkeys talking and racing from tree to tree, frightening in their turn birds who were taking their afternoon rest. What a din of screeching birds and howling monkeys!

In the meantime the defeated cub came home to his mother, for that day father and sister had gone off by themselves, and there they lay together near the drinking pond, mother licking and patting him. But on these and several other occasions that followed the parents never interfered nor helped the children. It is the first requisite of a tiger's life that he should tackle his job, whether hunting or wandering, singly. At a certain time, in order to train them in self reliance, the parents put their cubs in the way of work, but nothing more.

At last it rained so hard that I lost sight of them for more than a fortnight. It was about the beginning of August while the postman and I had gone across to the village of Sundari for the mail, that we heard of four tigers there who had killed three head of cattle in a week. This whetted my curiosity, and as soon as the mail was received the postman and I set out for the jungle. It did not take us long to find and recognize the family. The cubs had grown by now, the boy was almost as high as the mother, though not as long, his footprints resembled hers so closely that you could not distinguish them. Only one thing betrayed the cub, his step was not so long as the mother's. She took much wider strides. So when we saw two sets of identical pugs, with four in each of greater compass, we concluded that mother and son walked beside each other, while the daughter invariably kept the company of her father.

Having sighted their lairs, I went back to Tajjabpore with the postman. Then I hastened back to my four striped beasts. They moved ever closer to our village. In a couple of days they had come perilously dose to it. As they emerged from the thick jungle I perceived that all was not going well with the family. The father was becoming increasingly jealous of the son. Every time the mother's back was turned, the old fellow attacked the boy with the intent to kill. At one time he came so close to slashing the boy's throat with his paw that the latter yelled for help. Then from nowhere leaped mother between them, and attacked her husband. They fought and fought, but at last she won. After that severe tussle he ran away—never to be seen again.

Her job was now doubly difficult; she had to kill both for her two children and herself. But you know a tigress! She took no half measures; she forced the boy to fill his father's place, and he had to go and stalk the prey while mother waited at a given point to leap and kill.

One afternoon dose to nightfall they changed plan. She and daughter did the stalking. They brought a big buffalo up to him and lo, he leaped! But instead of falling on its neck, he fell on its rear, and with a terrific kick of his legs the black bull cleared himself and ran. Not one of the three could catch him, so that night they went without food. Next evening the same thing happened, but when on the fourth occasion the mother and daughter drove up to him half a dozen big buffaloes whom he could not attack, the mystery of the situation cleared. She was giving him his last lesson. After this the family would break up, so he must learn to stalk and kill all by himself. What was most surprising, she was giving him the hardest thing to do first, but by failure at the great one he was learning the easier tasks with infallible power and skill. How different that is from our human way of training people, with the easiest always first. In nature animals cannot afford such long drawn-out step-by-step training. Animal children cannot be segregated in the schoolroom from the sharp experiences of life. They have to be educated in the heart of life itself. The easy and the difficult befall them without any sequence. It is a pity that in civilization man has made the business of education so sequestered and slow.

However, to return to our tiger reaching his final initiation. I have already intimated that all three of them had gone without food for four days. Hunger was tearing their vitals. They were so famished that they curtailed their daylight sleep. Sister and brother, the fifth day, killed a baby monkey at the water hole. But it could not assuage their hunger. Late that afternoon when the sun was setting, they came out towards our village on the river bank and sat there looking at the bars of light vibrate and die on the high waters of the night of the full moon. In the village men and women sang as they finished their day's work, and Papias (Indian thrushes) sang in the sky—pa...p...i...a...! The green jungle throbbed like an emerald cast in a garnet crucible.

How swiftly the tropical twilight passes! In a half hour the moon had risen, sending currents of cold white fire through the waters and every bough of the trees. The three beasts of prey prowled around the village. But no cattle had gone astray, and men carrying torches were the only living creatures who passed and repassed on the roads. One of these men was myself. Seeing us, the tigers retreated from the village into the woods. I too went thither after putting out my torch, but circuitously. Hardly had I reached the edge of the jungle than I heard something start. With the celerity of an ape I went up a tree, and looking down I saw a milk-white buck going to graze on the ripe crop of the fields. Save his horns, the most of him was lost in the tall rice plants whose tops shivered in silver dance rhythms as he pushed through them. The moonlight was so bright that most animals could not sleep. Talk, talk, talk of birds and beasts rang like an insistent hammering on every nerve centre of one's body.

Slowly appeared against the wind a pair of emeralds. It was a tiger's eyes. He came up rapidly towards the rice crop in which the buck had buried himself. But all the time he kept closely under the shadow of the jungle. His purpose was to approach gradually until he reached the spot exactly behind the stag which would cut off the latter's retreat. Those green eyes grew larger, then vanished. In a short time an odour of tiger, carried up by the slow breeze, told me that he was crouching under my tree. I knew because of the jungle noises that the greedy buck, lost in rice-eating, had not heard his approach. Afar off on the other side were coming down wind four green eyes. In a short time the stag sensed the odour of tiger. He turned round and dashed for the jungle. Alas, poor brother—that moment from almost six feet away leaped a silvery flash which coiled itself around and hung from his neck. In two more minutes his throat was torn, and life had oozed out of him. Just then mother and sister leaped forward and claimed their share of the booty. But they were greeted with a sky-rending roar from the boy, that said: 'It is my kill. I did it all alone. I am the Master! I am the King!' Mother had apparently had previous experience in initiating children. She thrust a paw at sister who still insisted on claiming her share, and stilled her whining; then the two of them slunk away out of sight.

After he had eaten his fill, the cub roared and yelled as he went in the direction of the water hole. His cry of triumph told all the world that he had graduated from school. The far off panic-stricken echoes shouted, 'Here comes the King of the beasts.'

Now mother and daughter emerged from the shadows and fell upon the remains of the dead buck. They ate long and well. After all, they had to feed the hunger of nearly a week.

From that night on, we saw no more triple pugmarks. For several days we noticed a solitary tiger's track in the deep jungles, and the other two, the mother and daughter, went in the opposite direction, no doubt looking for father near some village up the river. Thus ends the story of a tiger's initiation. Not only they, but all other animals perform a series of rites which teaches them self-control and self-reliance with which they may be trusted to live their life.

The Tiger and the Woodcutter

WILLIAM FREDERICK TRAVERS O'CONNOR

Once upon a time there were two tigers who lived in a forest and had a family of three children. The Father Tiger grew old and began to fail, and just before his death he sent for his three children and addressed them as follows:

'Remember, my children,' said he, 'that the Tiger is Lord of the jungle; he roams about at his will and makes a prey of the other animals as he wishes, and none can gainsay him. But there is one animal against whom you must be on your guard. He alone is more powerful and cunning than the Tiger. That animal is Man, and I warn you solemnly before I die to beware of Man, and on no account to try to hunt or to kill him.'

So saying, the old Tiger turned on his side and died.

The three young tigers listened respectfully to the words of their dying parent and promised to obey; and the elder brothers, who were obedient sons, were careful to follow his advice. They confined their attentions to the slaughter of deer, pigs, and other denizens of the forest, and were careful, whenever they came within sight or scent of any human being, to clear off as fast as they could from so dangerous a neighbourhood. But the youngest Tiger was of an independent and inquisitive disposition. As he grew older and stronger he began to chafe against the restriction that had been imposed upon him.

'What, after all,' thought he to himself, 'can be this creature Man that I should not slay him if I wish. I am told that he is but a defenceless creature, that his strength cannot be compared to mine, and that his claws and teeth are quite contemptible. I can pull down the largest stag or tackle the fiercest boar with impunity. Why, then, should not I be able to kill and eat Man also?'

So after a while, in his conceit and folly, he determined to quit his own part of the forest and to venture forth towards the open country in search of a Man as his prey. His two brothers and his mother tried to reason with him and to persuade him to remember the words of his dying father, but with no avail; and finally, one fine morning, in spite of their prayers and entreaties, he set off alone on his search.

He had not proceeded very far when he met an old, worn-out pack-Bullock, thin and emaciated, and with the marks of many ancient scars on his back. The young Tiger had never seen a Bullock before, and he regarded the creature with some curiosity. Walking up to it he said:

'What sort of animal are you, pray? Are you a Man by any chance?'

'No, indeed,' replied the creature; 'I am only a poor Bullock.'

'Ah!' said the Tiger. 'Well, perhaps you can tell me what sort of an animal Man is, for I am just going out to find and kill one.'

'Beware of Man, young Tiger,' replied the Bullock; 'he is a dangerous and a faithless creature. Just look at me for example. From the time when I was very young I was Man's servant. I carried loads for him on my back, as you may see by these scars, and for many years I slaved for him faithfully and well. While I was young and strong he cared for me and valued me highly; but as soon as I became old and weak, and was no longer able to do his work, he turned me out into this wild jungle to seek my food as best I might, and gave no thought for me in my old age. I warn you solemnly to leave him alone and not to try and kill him. He is very cunning and dangerous.'

But the young Tiger only laughed at the warning and went on his way. Soon afterwards he came across an ancient Elephant wandering by itself on the outskirts of the forest, and feeding with its trunk on the grasses and foliage which it loves. The old animal had a wrinkled skin and a small and bleary eye, and behind its huge ears were many cuts and ancient scars, showing where the goad had been so frequently applied.

The young Tiger eyed this strange animal with some surprise, and going up to it he said:

'What sort of an animal are you, please? You are not a Man, I suppose?'

'No, indeed,' replied the Elephant, 'I am only a poor old worn-out Elephant.'

'Is that so?' answered the Tiger. 'Perhaps you can tell me, however, what sort of a creature Man is, as I am now hunting for one in order to kill and eat him.'

'Beware how you hunt Man, young Tiger,' replied the old Elephant; 'he is a faithless and dangerous animal. Look at my case. Although I am the Lord of the jungle, Man tamed me, and trained me, and made me his servant for many years. He put a saddle on my back and made stirrups of my ears, and he used to strike me over my head with an iron goad. While I was young and strong he valued me highly. Food was brought to me, as much as I could eat every day, and I had a special attendant who used to wash and groom me, and to see to all my wants. But when I became old and too infirm for further work, he turned me out into the jungle to fend for myself as best I could. If you will take my advice you will leave Man alone, or it will be the worse for you in the end.'

But the young Tiger laughed contemptuously and went on his way. After proceeding for some little distance he heard the sound of someone chopping wood, and creeping near he saw that it was a Woodcutter engaged in felling a tree. After watching him for some time the Tiger emerged from the jungle, and going up to the Man, he asked what sort of an animal he was. The Woodcutter replied:

'Why, what an ignorant Tiger you are; can't you see that I am a Man?'

'Oh, are you,' replied the Tiger, 'what a piece of luck for me. I was just looking for a Man in order to kill and eat him, and you will do nicely.'

On hearing this the Woodcutter began to laugh.

'Kill and eat *me*,' he replied, 'why, don't you know that Man is much too clever to be killed and eaten by a Tiger? Just come with me a little way and I will show you some things which only a Man knows, but which will be very useful for you to learn.'

The Tiger thought that this was a good idea, so he followed the Man through the jungle until they came to the Man's house, which was strongly built of timber and heavy logs.

'What is that place?' said the Tiger when he saw it.

'That is called a house,' replied the Man. 'I will show you how we use it.'

And so saying he went inside and shut the door.

'Now,' said he, speaking from the inside to the Tiger, 'you see what a foolish creature a Tiger is compared to a Man. You poor animals live in a hole in the forest, exposed to wind, rain, cold and heat; and all your strength is of no value to make a house like this. Whereas I, although I am so much weaker than you, can build myself a fine house, where I live at my ease, indifferent to the weather and secure from the attacks of wild animals.'

On hearing this the young Tiger flew into a violent passion.

'What right,' said he, 'has an ugly, defenceless creature like you to possess such a lovely house? Look at me, with my beautiful stripes, and my great teeth and claws, and my long tail. I am far more worthy than you of a house. Come out at once, and give your house over to me.'

‘Oh, very well,’ said the Man, and he came out of the house leaving the door open, and the Tiger stalked in.

‘Now, look at me,’ called out the conceited young Tiger from inside, ‘don’t I look nice in my fine house?’

‘Very nice indeed,’ replied the Man, and bolting the door outside he walked off with his axe, leaving the Tiger to starve to death.

TIGER.

Tiger and Elephant

JAMES MCINTYRE

On Ganges banks roams the tiger,
And lion rules by the Niger,
Hunter heard shrill cry of peacocks,
In Indian jungles go in flocks.
And he saw tiger crouch and spring,
To crush a bird with beauteous wing,
But the tiger missed his aim,
And he hung his head with shame.
Then there came a mighty crush,
Of elephants rush through the bush,
The tiger cat-like crouched on ground,
And elephants rushed in with bound.
In front was baby elephant,
To crush its bones did tiger want,
But mother saw fierce forest ranger,
And she gave a cry of danger.

Leader of herd he madly rushed,
Resolved the tiger should be crushed,
But tiger strove to run away,
Willing to relinquish prey.
But when he found that he must fight,
On elephant's back he strove to light,
But elephant struck him with his foot,
And then with tusks he did him root.
So now once more must praise be sung;
To beasts who nobly fight for young,
And grateful feelings were now stirred,
Towards the leader of the herd.

The Palki and the Tiger

MAHARANI SUNITY DEVI

In a lonely village in the Hazaribagh district the peaceful dwellers were one evening disturbed by shrill cries of distress. When they gathered round the house from whence the cries came, they discovered that a ghastly murder had been committed. The headman of the village immediately despatched two messengers for the police. These men started in the dawn and reached the Police outpost just before sunset.

The Inspector-in-charge was a Bengalee, named Bose, who was a very intelligent officer and keen on his work. As soon as he received information of the murder, he ordered one of his staff to arrange for a *push-push* (carriage which is partly drawn and partly pushed by men) and a set of bearers. He quickly put together a few requisites for the journey, and was soon ready. The night was not far advanced when the orderly returned with a *push-push* and eight bearers, and Bose started off, attended by his cook and body-servant.

The road lay through a forest. At times the path was so narrow and rocky that the men could make little progress, and at last they declared that the road was impassable for a wheeled conveyance, and that it was necessary for the Inspector to change into a palki. One of them said that about two miles off the road there was a village, and that in the village there lived a rich Hindustani merchant who might lend a palki. Bose was pleased at the suggestion and told the *push-push* bearers to take him to the village. They needed no second bidding, and the Inspector was soon being trundled across the paddy fields that lay between the village and the road. Arrived there, he hastened to the merchant's house and asked to see him.

A handsome up-countryman came out and when, he saw that his visitor was a gentleman he courteously asked him to enter and be seated.

The Inspector soon explained his necessity for a palki, and the rich man placed his at the disposal of the police officer. 'But Jenab (Sir),' he said, 'tigers are bad in this forest and you have to pass through a part known to be a favourite haunt of theirs. Have you any fire-arms?'

'Only my revolver,' said Bose 'but I must push on and take my chance.' And as the palki now stood ready and the bearers declared themselves refreshed, he thanked his host for his ready assistance, bade him farewell and started once again.

The bearers were full of spirits after their rest at the merchant's house and for a mile or two travelled at a rapid pace; but the narrow winding road impeded their progress, and as the night advanced the eerie sounds of the forest must have got on their nerves. At the commencement of the journey they had beguiled the march with stories of tigers and bears met in the forest, but after some hours of travel they became silent; and beyond the usual directions of the forward men concerning the road and occasionally a shrill cry to scare away wild animals, they made no remarks to each other.

Within the palki, Bose lay fitfully dozing. The night was oppressive and his thoughts were on the murder and his chances of a successful capture of the wrong-doer. The road had become wider and level and the men were going along at a good pace, when suddenly they dropped the palki to the ground and fled in all directions. Bose shouted: 'What is up? Why have you run away?' No answer greeted his ears but a strange odour penetrated his nostrils and he knew there was a tiger in the jungle. He quickly pulled the doors of the palki jamming them as securely as he could with the ends of his razai (quilt). Then he tore the strong border off his dhoti (loin cloth) and commenced to bind the handles of the doors together. He had just finished firmly lashing together the handles on one side when he heard an ominous growling. With frantic haste he bound the handles of the opposite doors together, praying fervently that he might escape the jaws of the tiger.

The animal continued growling. Evidently the dark bulk of the palki frightened him. Bose sat inside, huddled in a heap and breathless. The tiger, re-assured by the stillness of the object before him, ceased growling; and presently, the soft thud of his feet and his sniffing round the palki told the trembling man within that 'Stripes' was making an investigation.

Now a mighty roar shook the jungles and Bose realized that the tiger had leapt upon the roof of the palki and was scratching furiously at it. Bose clutched the handles of the doors and held on to them with the grip of despair. The tiger scratched and growled and finally bounded off the top and began a vigorous assault upon the side. The palki toppled over on to its other side. Poor Bose congratulated himself that now one of the doors rested upon Mother Earth and he could give his whole energy to defending the other. He gripped the handles with renewed determination and waited.

The tiger had sustained a shock at seeing the unknown monster he was tackling roll over, and for a time satisfied himself by growling savagely.

But as the monster lay still 'Stripes' tried the experiment of a sharp blow with his paw. The palki rested on uneven ground and the blow made it rock. The tiger waited awhile; and when the rocking had subsided administered another stroke. The palki rocked again. The situation now developed into a game between the huge cat and the palki. When he slapped the palki rocked; and when the palki ceased vibrating the tiger slapped again. Inside the palki, the Inspector held on to the handles of the door and prayed for deliverance.

At last the tiger, wearied of the game and purring loudly, walked away. Bose breathed more freely but knew not if the danger was past. There he lay gripping the handles of the door and wishing for daylight. At last the dawn broke and with the first rays of light courage returned to the bearers and servants, who were hiding in the branches of the surrounding trees. They called to each other, expressing anxiety as to their master's fate. Finally, as the daylight grew stronger they encouraged each other to descend and approach the palki.

As they examined it with wonder some very cutting remarks from within assured them of their master's existence, and with many apologies for the abrupt way in which they had abandoned him they righted the palki and assisted him out.

The journey was soon resumed and Bose had the satisfaction of arresting the murderer in spite of his ill-timed adventure and forced delay.

Eyes of the Tiger

BULBUL SHARMA

Have you ever looked into the eyes of a tiger? A living, breathing tiger? Well, I have, many, many years ago.

I was a young girl then and we lived in a town called Bhilai. It was a lonely, small town then with hardly any houses and a gigantic steel plant that towered over everything. Every time we had to catch a train to go anywhere, we had to travel through a dense forest to get to the big city of Nagpur, which was the major train station closest to Bhilai. I remember it always got dark as soon as our convoy of cars entered the most dense part of the forest. Why could we not leave Bhilai earlier? I often wondered but never dared to ask any of the adults.

Anyway, once there we were travelling on the narrow, bumpy road, tall trees forming a green wall on either side of us. We always travelled in an old jeep. It was uncomfortable and filled with diesel fumes but once in a while, I caught the delicious smell of poories and many other snacks which my mother always carried in a giant tiffin box. Every half an hour she would feed us something. 'Keep room for oranges in Nagpur,' my father would say.

Slowly the last rays of sunlight vanished and the trees changed from green to black as evening fell. I could hear an owl screech somewhere deep inside the forest. Suddenly, a family of hares ran across the road and our driver had to step on the brakes quickly, giving us all a jolt. The journey seemed endless, and tired of watching the road and the line of swaying dark shadows, I soon fell asleep.

I woke to someone shaking me and I heard my father's voice whispering in my ears. 'Wake up. Look.' I opened my eyes reluctantly and looked out. The jeep seemed to have stopped and its bright headlights lit up the entire road, making the tree trunks gleam like silver pillars. Then I saw the tiger standing in front of us.

It was looking straight at the jeep, its long whiskers twitching with anger, its golden eyes glittering in the bright light like two precious jewels. It was so near our jeep that I could see its eyes clearly.

We waited, holding our breath. The tiger waited, too, unsure of what to do. The jeep loaded with humans did not look like edible prey so there was no point of charging at it but this tin box was disturbing its territory so it should be taught a lesson.

As we watched, awestruck by its presence, the handsome, majestic creature opened its jaws and gave a mighty roar. The entire forest echoed with this powerful, thrilling sound. My heart was pounding with excitement, tinged with fear, and I held my father's hand tightly.

'Are the doors locked?' asked my mother.

'Shusssh,' hissed my father. 'Don't make a noise. You might annoy it more.'

The tiger peered into our jeep and then satisfied that it had given us a stern warning, it yawned, displaying its fearsome teeth and slowly walked away into the forest.

Later—many years later—we laughed about this. Would the locked doors have stopped the tiger from attacking us? We found out that this tiger always roamed around in this area of the forest and often slept in the old, ruined temple that was close by. There was a priest who lived there and he often left food for the tiger. The tiger seemed to like khichdi and fruit. Though I am sure he or she hunted many animals like deer and wild boar that formed its normal diet, because the tiger I saw that day, lit up in the car's headlights, looked very well fed and strong.

Then one day, many, many years later, the same tiger with the same eyes filled with rage, came into my room as I sat writing. I was shocked and could not believe my eyes. A tiger in the mountains of Simla was unheard of. I stared at the tiger and the tiger stared back at me. I was petrified as it started walking towards me slowly, stealthily as if stalking its prey. It raised its head and fixed a piercing, golden gaze on me. I swallowed, knowing it was going to attack me any minute. Closer and closer it came. I could not breathe. I just waited for the last terrifying moment when it would tear me to pieces. The furious eyes were so close that I could see the tiny flecks of gold in its pupils. Its nose, furry and wet, twitched like a kitten's and I suddenly began to laugh.

Here I was, about to be eaten up alive but I was laughing like an idiot. The tiger watched me and then smiled. Yes. It smiled with its long whiskers moving in a comical way. The eyes now shone with kindness.

I put a hand out and touched its forehead. The rough fur felt warm under my hand. I looked around to see if I could find any food to give the tiger. There was half a packet of potato chips lying on the table. I took some out and offered it to the tiger. I was a bit scared that it might bite my hand off but the tiger sniffed at the chips and took a few like a well-trained dog. Then it began munching, looking at me greedily, begging for some more treats just like my pet dog and I said, 'Good dog! Sit down.' For a moment I thought it would lie down and roll on its back like a dog wanting its stomach tickled. 'Good doggy,' I said again. The tiger stopped munching at once and gave me a shocked look.

‘I am sorry. I shouldn’t have called you a dog. I hope you don’t mind,’ I said. The tiger turned around and walked away, purring angrily, arching its back. It stopped near the door and turned its head to look at me. I saw to my surprise that it had turned into a white tiger—a very rare animal. Suddenly lightning flashed all around us and a bloodcurdling roar filled the room but for some strange reason, I did not feel frightened at all. The roar, so powerful and majestic, sounded wonderful. It was like thunder rolling over the high mountains. I wanted to hear it over and over again. I waited for the roar to come once more. Then the light in the room changed and my friend, the potato chips eating tiger, slowly turned into a trembling, silver shadow. With another roar, it vanished.

I ran out into the hillside, searching for it in the darkness but I could not see anything at all. I heard the roar again. The deodar trees began to sway, and suddenly a golden and black tiger’s head, appeared. It seemed to be smiling at me. I moved ahead and the head flew up with a roar and the body became a silver shadow.

I was left alone in the darkness but I could still hear the roar echoing in my ears. I could still feel the rough fur under my palm. I closed my eyes and knew the tiger was staring at me with its gold-specked, fiery eyes. Then it vanished into the darkness. I will never forget those magical kind eyes of my friendly tiger ghost. I am sure it will come to visit me again and that is why I have kept many packets of potato chips under my table.

The Home of the Tigers

S. EARDLEY-WILMOT

It was winter in northern India. A haze lay over the arid plains; its sharply defined line shewed the elevation beyond which the dust-laden air might not rise, and emphasized the purity of the clear, blue atmosphere above it. It was as if the toil of men and the sufferings of animals were purposely hidden from the abode of the gods. To the mortals below this straight line of haze formed a mysterious horizon, and its greyness was absorbed in the distance on either hand; but in the centre the sun was balanced like a fiery ball in a still lake of vivid orange.

The forest stood, silent and sombre, facing the sunset, and now a cool breeze arose and blew fitfully. Its coming could be heard like the murmuring of shallow but rapid waters.

First in the distance the tops of lightly poised bamboos swayed to and fro like green banners gently waved in warning; then the trees took up the challenge and rustled stiffly, while a few withered leaves fluttered in spirals to the earth; lastly the drying grasses bent their heads, protesting with soft shiverings. The chilly air passed away towards the south, and there was silence until the next sigh from the mountains reached the forest.

The land was one of tall trees and giant grasses, of running streams, and of deep ravines with clear-cut banks. Here the vegetation held sway over the waters. During the monsoon the turbid torrents revenged themselves for the restraint of the past months by widening the watercourses and uprooting such trees as came within their reach; but during the rest of the year the luxuriant growth of grass and timber asserted itself; it seized on every vacant spot and fortified it with wide-spread roots against the next attack of the enemy.

Now the rivers were quiescent in their sandy beds, and between the rocks and boulders only a faint trickle of water poured into the pools that the floods had deeply scoured. In these pools were great fish, entrapped till the next mountain storm should send them release; they lay motionless in infinite patience. From time to time the birds of the waters came to visit them; the white-capped robin displayed his harmonious plumage of indigo and chestnut; the fork-tail, in handsome dress of black and white, perched on a boulder to utter his joyous song, or the blue thrush whistled his sweet notes as he hurried past.

In one such watercourse an island had withstood a century of successive floods; a few trees stood high above the tall grasses and their spreading boughs looked down on the impenetrable tangle, with here and there a glimpse of the solid earth. In a slight depression in the soil lay three puny, helpless kittens with clouded blue eyes, big ears and enormous paws; a glance at their yellow bodies, striped with black, permitted no doubt of their parentage, even were it not that close at hand there reclined, in the watchful sleep common to all wild animals, a handsome well-marked tigress of unusual size. To one side lay a hollow log, the remains of an ancient stem from the thick forest that clothed each bank of the stream.

The sun was now low in the west; the evening breeze had become more persistent and the resistance of the vegetation to it more audible. A slight mist was forming in the low ground, and, as it rose above the sheltering banks, it was torn away and floated southwards in the air currents. The birds were passing on their homeward flight or were settling themselves in their roosting places with much rustling of feathers, with gentle chirpings, or with angry scoldings, according to their family habits. The cubs commenced to whine and to stray aimlessly over the trampled grass raising their paws high at each step and staggering with the weakness of unaccustomed muscles, and then too the tigress arose and yawned widely, her head bowed between distended paws. She collected her family by picking up each cub in her mouth and lay down beside them till contented murmurings were followed by the sleep of repletion. Then, again picking up her cubs, she pushed them into the mouth of the hollow log and stood looking around her, for the time of hunting had already arrived.

Within a few inches of nine feet in length and standing some three feet high at the shoulders, the pure black and white of her markings and the clear red of her colouring were especially noticeable, as well as the lissom strength of her supple body that gave promise of quickness and agility. Then, as the short twilight of the East faded away and darkness fell on the earth, though the sky was still luminous with dying colours, she seemed to be swallowed up in the evening gloom as she moved noiselessly into the forest. At first she appeared to have no defined purpose, to be awaiting guidance from any chance sound that might reach her ears. And so she strolled on for miles, avoiding the denser patches of cover, standing sometimes to listen intently, and losing no warning that the sighs of the jungle might afford. When the brown night-jars lay crouched on the faded leaves, uttering their monotonous notes, it was to the tigress a proof that nothing was lurking in her path; when they suddenly rose and, wheeling, displayed their white wing-spots, she halted to learn the reason of their flight. Even the creaking of the bamboo stems as they rubbed together brought her to a standstill, and, when a dry branch snapped with its own weight and fell with a dull blow upon the earth, she had crouched at its first movement and did not again stand erect till, after several minutes of careful inspection, she was persuaded that there was no cause for anxiety. She had, in short, to keep every sense continually on the alert with a view both to self-preservation and to success in hunting.

And thus feeling the pangs of hunger more pronounced as each hour passed, she struck at length a narrow footpath running at right angles to her course. The dew was dripping heavily from the trees as she stood undecided whether to turn to right or left, then, making up her mind, she stepped on to the track, keeping to its darkest side and approaching each bend and turning with slow precision that augured ill for any that might be coming that way. Her footsteps were noiseless on the beaten footway.

Suddenly the tigress stopped and lay crouching on her belly, motionless save for the nervous twitching of her tail that lay snake-like along the path. At some distance ahead slight movements were audible in the forest, footsteps amongst the dead leaves, a rustling in the tall grasses, even a sound of foliage being torn from the branches; but all so indistinct as to render almost impossible any decision as to their origin. The tigress during her long walk had seen no living animal. From a distance several times had come the alarm cry of the spotted-deer, and once a sounder of pig had rushed through the forest as the breeze bore the scent of a dangerous enemy to their nostrils. She had been unlucky in having the game down-wind on each occasion, and, now that she was more favourably situated, she could not recognize the sounds she heard; she knew only that they were too gentle for the movements of an elephant through the forest, and too noisy for those of a grazing porcupine, the two extremes of the wildlife around that at that moment possessed an interest for her.

But the wind, eddying over the forest, brought the information that neither eyes nor ears could afford; it whispered that there were deer ahead, and she responded with drawn lips and a little sigh of satisfaction. A few moments later a sambhar stag stood on the path browzing on the foliage, and from time to time petulantly, thrashing the overhanging boughs with his horns; for the rutting reason was long past and the dead antlers were pressing on the living burrs, so that an unpleasant tickling urged him to rid himself of this constant annoyance. The stag was in the prime of his strength. His massive horns swept in a forty-inch curve to either side, and the long brow-antlers and the two tines on top were sharp and white from constant use. His hide was covered with patches of mud where he had wallowed to rid himself of the pest of midday insects, and long, black hair hung from his throat that was scarred from a hundred fights. His huge ears were never still, and the deep, black eyes were keenly on the alert.

The tigress' chance had come, and it depended now chiefly on her skill whether or not she would secure a meal. She rose and hurried down the narrow path with stealthy, sinuous strides; but for the time luck was against her, and the crackle of a broken twig under her fore-paw sounded loud and clear in the still night. The noise startled the stag and sent him off at a hand gallop; not for two or three hundred yards did he stop, and even then remained thoroughly suspicious. The path here skirted a deep declivity, and at its foot a small watercourse glimmered faintly in the light of a rising moon. The opposite banks were of inky blackness, all detail being obliterated; only the general direction of the ravine was indicated in a light so dim that it seemed merely to intensify the darkness of the shadows. As the stag stood, uneasy and uncertain of the course he should pursue, a quick thudding of feet renewed his alarm; he turned to spring down the slope and seek safety in the turns and bends of the rivulet when he was struck as by a thunderbolt and, rolling over and over in a cloud of dust and gravel, lay with a broken neck, damming up the water with his heavy body.

The tigress at first crouched beside her victim, trembling with the excitement of the hunt and furious at the pain of the bruises she had received in the headlong fall; for she had not quitted her hold of an animal of nearly twice her weight until it lay dead beneath her. She watched the stag with eyes that seemed to burn with a crimson flame, and from time to time uttered low growls, as if to express a longing for any interference that might give opportunity to vent her rage; then, rising, she seized the sambhar roughly by the neck and shook it till the antlers rattled on the stones, finally dragging it into the heavy cover on the banks of the stream. From this retreat a tearing of flesh, a crunching of bones and ill-tempered snarls plainly proved that she was satisfying her appetite.

The moon was high when she again appeared and drank deeply from the running water; then, three times in succession, at intervals of about a minute, she uttered roars that echoed through the forest and were thrown back from the hills. The first reply came almost immediately in the alarm cry of the spotted-deer and in the grunts of frightened monkeys, even the peacocks from their high perches joined in the warnings uttered for the benefit of all the forest-folk. Later came in an answering roar, the signal she was expecting, and she quietly waited, occasionally giving a low moaning cry to direct the guest she had invited to the feast

The stream now lay glittering in the moonlight, its sandy banks defined in brilliant white, and at a distance a vague movement could be detected, ceasing where the shadows lay more pronounced in the rays of the moon. It was as if a silver snake was undulating in a mysterious course, a phenomenon weird and inexplicable that laid a grip on the heart of the fear of the unknown. But the tigress still appeared to be indifferent; she was ostentatiously engaged in removing from her coat the signs of the recent struggle and of the feast that had followed, nor did she look up when a tiger stood on the sand-bank before her, or admire the effect of the moonbeams which converted his sleek back into shining metal, while his massive limbs seemed carved out of ebony in the deep shadow thrown by his body.

His colouring was not so vivid as that of his mate, but she looked almost a weakling by his side; his deep ruff made his head appear ponderous, and on his shoulders the supple skin moved tightly over the rounded masses of muscle. He greeted the tigress with that quiet retraction of the lips which in the cat tribe is made to do duty for the expression of many emotions, and is unmistakable even by dull human beings should they be given opportunity to translate it in conjunction with the silent eloquence of the eyes. She moved away into the forest; for tigers have this one thing in common with the natives of India that they will not eat in the company of their females, preferring a solitary repast.

In a listless manner she wandered towards her lair, somewhat oppressed by her heavy meal, not again to be tempted to the hunt, though not omitting to mark the direction taken by deer or pig as they passed in the moonlight; till, as the daylight was again spreading over the forest, she stood by the hollow log and answered gently to the impatient whinings of her hungry cubs. They struggled towards her, stumbling as they came, and her eyes now shone kindly with a yellow light in marked contrast to her looks as she lay a few hours ago beside her victim. She had suckled her family, had made their toilets, had even replaced them in the hollow log, and was dozing beside the entrance to the nursery before heavy footsteps proclaimed the arrival of the tiger, gorged with flesh, and wanting nothing but repose after the feast that had followed on many hours of fruitless hunting. Then the whole family, happy in their lives and in their surroundings, slept without awakening until far into the noontide.

The Foolish Tiger
(A Panchatantra Story)

FLORA ANNIE STEEL

Once upon a time a tiger was caught in a trap. He tried in vain to get out through the bars, and rolled and bit with rage and grief when he failed.

By chance a poor Brahman came by. 'Let me out of this cage, O pious one!' cried the tiger.

'Nay, my friend,' replied the Brahman mildly, 'you would probably eat me if I did.'

'Not at all!' swore the tiger with many oaths, 'On the contrary, I should be forever grateful, and serve you as a slave.'

Now, when the tiger sobbed and sighed and wept and swore, the pious Brahman's heart softened, and at last he consented to open the door of the cage. Out popped the tiger, and, seizing the poor man, cried, 'What a fool you are! What is to prevent my eating you now, for after being cooped up so long I am just terribly hungry?'

In vain the Brahman pleaded for his life; the most he could gain was a promise to abide by the decision of the first three things he chose to question as to the justice of the tiger's action.

So the Brahman first asked a pipal tree what it thought of the matter, but the pipal tree replied coldly, 'What have you to complain about? Don't I give shade and shelter to every one who passes by, and don't they in return tear down my branches to feed their cattle? Don't whimper—be a man!'

Then the Brahman, sad at heart, went further afield till he saw a buffalo turning a well-wheel; but he fared no better from it, for it answered: 'You are a fool to expect gratitude! Look at me! While I gave milk they fed me on cotton-seed and oil-cake, but now I am dry they yoke me here, and give me refuse as fodder!'

The Brahman, still more sad, asked the road to give him its opinion.

'My dear sir,' said the road, 'how foolish you are to expect anything else! Here am I, useful to everybody, yet all, rich and poor, great and small, trample on me as they go past, giving me nothing but the ashes of their pipes and the husks of their grain!'

On this the Brahman turned back sorrowfully, and on the way he met a jackal, who called out, 'Why, what's the matter, Mr Brahman? You look as miserable as a fish out of water!'

The Brahman told him all that had occurred. 'How very confusing,' said the jackal, when the recital was ended, 'would you mind telling me over again, for everything seems so mixed up?'

The Brahman told it all over again, but the jackal shook his head in a distracted sort of way, and still could not understand.

'It's very odd,' said he sadly, 'but it all seems to go in at one ear and out at the other! I will go to the place where it all happened, and then, perhaps, I shall be able to give a judgment.'

So they returned to the cage, by which the tiger was waiting for the Brahman, and sharpening his teeth and claws.

'You've been away a long time!' growled the savage beast, 'but now let us begin our dinner.'

'*Our* dinner!' thought the wretched Brahman, as his knees knocked together with fright, 'What a remarkably delicate way of putting it!'

'Give me five minutes, my lord!' he pleaded, 'In order that I may explain matters to the jackal here, who is somewhat slow in his wits.'

The tiger consented, and the Brahman began the whole story over again, not missing a single detail, and spinning as long a yarn as possible.

'Oh, my poor brain! Oh, my poor brain!' cried the jackal, wringing its paws. 'Let me see! How did it all begin? You were in the cage, and the tiger came walking by—'

'Pooh!' interrupted the tiger, 'What a fool you are! I was in the cage.'

'Of course!' cried the jackal, pretending to tremble with fright, 'Yes! I was in the cage—no, I wasn't—dear! Dear! Where are my wits? Let me see—the tiger was in the Brahman, and the cage came walking by—no, that's not it, either! Well, don't mind me, but begin your dinner, for I shall never understand!'

'Yes, you shall!' returned the tiger, in a rage at the jackal's stupidity, 'I'll *make* you understand! Look here—I am the tiger—'

'Yes, my lord!'

'And that is the Brahman—'

'Yes, my lord!'

'And that is the cage—'

'Yes, my lord!'

'And I was in the cage—do you understand?'

'Yes—no—please, my lord—'

'Well?' cried the tiger impatiently.

'Please, my lord! How did you get in?'

'How? Why in the usual way, of course!'

'Oh, dear me! My head is beginning to whirl again! Please don't be angry, my lord, but what is the usual way?'

At this the tiger lost patience, and jumping into the cage, cried, 'This way! Now do you understand how it was?'

'Perfectly!' grinned the jackal, as he dexterously shut the door, 'And if you will permit me to say so, I think matters will remain as they were!'

The Tiger

ELLA WHEELER WILCOX

In the still jungle of the senses lay
A tiger soundly sleeping, till one day
A bold young hunter chanced to come that way.
'How calm,' he said, 'that splendid creature lies,
I long to rouse him into swift surprise!'
The well aimed arrow shot from amorous eyes,
And lo! the tiger rouses up and turns,
A coal of fire his glowing eyeball burns,
His mighty frame with savage hunger yearns.
He crouches for a spring; his eyes dilate—
Alas! bold hunter, what shall be thy fate?
Thou canst not fly, it is too late, too late.
Once having tasted human flesh, ah! then,
Woe, woe unto the whole rash world of men,
The wakened tiger will not sleep again.

To See a Tiger

RUSKIN BOND

Mr Kishore, my neighbour, drove me out to the forest rest house in his jeep, told me he'd be back in two days, and left me in the jungle. The caretaker of the rest house, a retired Indian Army corporal, made me a cup of tea.

'You have come to see the animals, sir?'

'Yes,' I said, looking around the clearing in front of the house, where a few domestic fowls scrabbled in the dust. 'Will I have to go far?'

'This is the best place, sir,' said the caretaker. 'See, the river is just below.'

A stream of clear mountain water ran through a shady glade of sal and shisham trees about fifty yards from the house.

'The animals come at night,' said the caretaker. 'You can sit in the veranda, with a cup of tea, and watch them. You must be very quiet, of course.'

'Will I see a tiger?' I asked. 'I've come to see a tiger.'

'Perhaps the tiger will come, sir,' said the caretaker with a tolerant smile. 'He will do his best, I am sure.'

He made me a simple lunch of rice and lentils, flavoured with a mango pickle. I spent the afternoon with a book taken from the rest house bookshelf. The small library hadn't been touched for over twenty years, and I had to make my choice from Marie Corelli, P.C. Wren, and early Wodehouse. I plumped for a Wodehosue—*Love among the Chickens*. A peacock flaunted its tail feathers on the lawn, but I was not distracted. I had seen plenty of peacocks.

When it grew dark, I took up my position in the veranda, on an old cane chair. Bhag Singh, the caretaker, brought me dinner on a brass thali (tray), two different vegetables in separate katoris (brass bowls). The chapaties came in relays, brought hot from the kitchen by Bhag Singh's ten-year-old son. Then, sustained by more tea, sweet and milky, I began my vigil. It took an hour for Bhag Singh's family to settle down for the night in their outhouse. Their pi-dog stood outside, barking at me for half an hour, before he too fell asleep. The moon came up over the foothills, and the stream could be seen quite clearly.

And then a strange sound filled the night air. Not the roar of a tiger, nor the sawing of a leopard, but a rising crescendo of noise—wurk, wurk, wurk—issuing from the muddy banks near the stream. All the frogs in the jungle seemed to have gathered there that night. They must have been having a sort of an old boys' reunion, because everyone seemed to have something to say for himself. The speeches continued for about an hour. Then the meeting broke up, and silence returned to the forest.

A jackal slunk across the clearing. A puff of wind brushed through the trees. I was almost asleep when a cicada burst into violent music in a nearby tree. I started, and stared out at the silver, moon-green stream; but no animals came to drink that night.

The next evening Bhag Singh offered to sit up with me. He placed a charcoal burner on the veranda, and topped it with a large basin of tea.

'Whenever you feel sleepy, sir, I'll give you a glass of tea.'

Did we hear a panther—or was someone sawing wood? The sounds are similar, in the distance. The frogs started up again. The old boys must have brought their wives along this time, because instead of speeches there was general conversation, exactly like the natter of a cocktail party.

By morning I had drunk over fifteen cups of tea. Out of respect for my grandfather, a pioneer tea planter in India, I did not complain. Bhag Singh made me an English breakfast—toast, fried eggs, and more tea.

The third night passed in much the same way, except that Bhag Singh's son stayed up with us and drank his quota of tea.

In the morning, Mr Kishore came for me in his jeep. 'Did you see anything?'

'A jackal,' I said.

'Never mind, you'll have better luck next time. Of course, the jungles aren't what they used to be...'

I said goodbye to Bhag Singh, and got into the jeep.

We had gone barely a hundred yards along the forest road when Mr Kishore brought the jeep to a sudden, jolting halt.

Right in the middle of the road, about thirty yards in front of us, stood a magnificent full-grown tiger.

The tiger didn't roar. He didn't even snarl. But he gave us what appeared to be a quick, disdainful glance, and then walked majestically across the road and into the jungle.

'What luck!' exclaimed Mr Kishore. 'You can't complain now, can you? You've seen your tiger!'

'Yes,' I said, 'three sleepless nights, and I've seen it in broad daylight!'

'Very considerate of the tiger,' laughed Mr Kishore, and drove on.

Tiger, Tiger, Who Are You

ADITI DE

In a little village in northern Kerala, there lived a man and his wife in a thatched mud house on the banks of a swirling river. Though they belonged to the struggling Pulaya community, who worked in the paddy fields and practiced herbal medicine, the villagers regarded the man almost as a demigod—for he was an expert in Kalaripayattu, the fast-paced martial art of the region, known for its eighteen basic styles or adavus.

'Have you heard of our champion's mastery of the thirteenth adavu?' the village masseur would ask the grain dealer, as they bathed in the communal pond at dawn, scrubbing off the herbal oils that made their dusky skins glisten. 'Even the raja holds him in high esteem,' the dealer responded. 'He's never been defeated in our part of the world. I believe he's unbeatable...'

Thanks to his Kalaripayattu skills, the reputation of this martial arts expert spread way beyond his village. Even the local king commanded his presence whenever a champion warrior from another kingdom posed a challenge.

One morning, the king's messenger arrived at the doorstep of the champion, summoning him to court at once. The expert brushed the soil from the fields off his hands, donned a much-washed mundu-veshti, and sped back with the messenger.

Bowing before the king, the expert waited. 'A champion from a neighbouring court is sure his Kalaripayattu skills are superior to yours,' revealed the king. 'I sent back a message that he had to match his words with his martial skills. Prepare for a bout in three days' time...'

Back home, the champion prepared himself for a ritual fast. To sustain him through it, his wife fed him a nourishing meal of gruel-like rice kanji with a koottu of lentils and bittergourd.

Then, he retreated into their tiny inner chamber to concentrate on the battle to come, speaking to no one until the time was right.

The appointed day woke to birdsong, the buzzing of summer flies, and a morning shower from the skies. The expert had prayed to Sri Porkali, his paradevata or patron deity, to bless him. He sought the boon of a victory, sacrificing a chicken to her as an offering. She was the mother goddess who presided over Kalaripayattu. His wife, just bathed, her wet hair rippling down the back of her clean mundu, saw him off with prayers, hoping her husband would return safely after the bout.

The king was to take care of the champion during the tournament, providing him with assistants and masseurs. As the court's honoured guest, he would dine well and have a special room to himself for its duration.

At the arena outside the royal court, under the spread of a giant banyan tree, flags had been hoisted to proclaim the rival kings, whose Kalaripayattu champions would battle for their honour. The conch sounded its clarion call to combat, and a court musician began to beat on the upright chenda drum at a dizzying pace.

The expert was sure he would vanquish his opponent as he stepped into the arena. He had mastered the eighteen adavus of Kalaripayattu, and was the people's favourite beyond dispute. He adjusted his 42-foot long, red-and-black kachcha or waist garment, made of intricately woven virali-pattu or Patan silk from Gujarat, tightening its band so that it would steady him as he moved rapidly and surely through the bout. The special silk was regarded as a sacred fabric in the local shrine. Over it, he wound an urumi, a flexible steel sword as long as his outstretched arms, ready to uncoil at his touch.

Following rules that had governed the martial art since time immemorial, both champions knew the timekeeper would blow his conch at the end of the bout. But for the moment, the champion launched into the first adavu, advancing and circling, attacking and bypassing his opponent. However, he felt he had met his match at the end of the first day, for the challenge was as skilled as he, and would not retreat an inch. They fought in various adavus each day, without either of them winning or losing.

'Both champions seem equally skilled,' noted the court chronicler to the head cook, at sundown on the seventeenth day. 'I fear our raja will lose face if our expert lets him down,' noted the oil merchant, joining their conversation, tugging at his drooping moustaches in exasperation. 'The very idea makes me shudder. What shall I say when I visit our relatives in the neighbouring town?'

The fears of the villagers and courtiers were not unjustified. Move for move, strike for strike, stride for stride, the champion felt his opponent was his equal. Undefeated so far, his spirits ebbed lower and lower. Must he bow his head in shame before the king, the courtiers, and the villagers who were so proud of him?

Back at his room after dusk, still dusty and scarred by the tussle, he meditated over his next move. His assistants had prepared herbal medicinal oils for his daily massage. But he turned away from them.

Instead, he asked if they could summon his wife to meet him when the next day dawned. She had stayed behind at their village, praying for her husband's victory.

Anxious at this unusual summons, his wife reached the court early. The champion ensured that no courtiers or assistants accompanied him when he met her. Her questioning look and her silence spoke volumes to him.

At first, he was silent. When he looked up at last, his eyes were fiery, his hair a tangled cloud of black strands around his lean face.

'Today, I will have to try the eighteenth adavu to fight the challenger,' the champion said softly, as if speaking to himself. 'My opponent is a master in his own way.' His puzzled wife did not say a word.

Pausing, he continued, 'What should I do if I can't best him with this last adavu? He's as sleekly muscled and quick-thinking as I am. I can't let our king down before his opponents. I have to win this bout.'

'I believe no other Kalaripayattu expert can get the better of you,' she reassured him. 'I am sure you will find another option.'

Absolute silence reigned for a while. Then, almost in a frenzy, he asked his wife, 'Will you make me a promise?'

'What is it?' she whispered.

'I haven't yet exhausted all the adavus I know. If this challenger refuses to be vanquished by the eighteenth adavu, I still have another alternative. I have to try an extraordinary adavu, a special one, rarely known even to kalari masters. As a youth, I learnt it from a guru in Tulunadu, not far away,' he confided. 'I have no other choice left. But I need your help...'

'How can I help?' she asked in distress, anxious about his plight.

'Through this adavu, called Almarattam, I can transform myself into another being. I should be able to conquer my challenger as a tiger,' he revealed, watching shadows of doubt flit across her face. 'But I will need your help to return to my normal form.'

He smiled at her confidently before continuing, 'This morning, all those watching the bout will expect us to use the eighteenth adavu. If I do not defeat the challenger this time.

I'll chant a secret mantra. Within seconds, my challenger will find himself face to face with a ferocious tiger. There's no way he can overcome me in this guise.'

'And then ...?' asked his wife.

'Once I have defeated him, I will not remain at the arena a moment longer. When I return home, you must follow my instructions closely,' the champion stressed. 'I'm going to teach you a mantra. You must chant it as soon as you catch sight of the tiger striding towards our hut and quickly use a broomstick to sprinkle cow dung, dissolved in water, on to its face. Make sure you do not miss. That will ensure that I return to my human form.'

She asked him to recite the mantra a hundred and one times. Each time, she repeated it after him, making sure she pronounced the words just right.

Finally, she tore herself away with a sigh to set out on the long and winding road to their village to await his return Thus reassured, the champion continued with preparations for the final bout.

The king, the courtiers and all the villagers gathered around the arena as early as they could. Some watchers-on from the neighbouring villages had also assembled, jostling for space around the ring. None of them could guess what was in store.

The challenger tightened his waistband, flexed his muscles, sleeked back his hair and roared, 'Where's your undefeated champion? I'm rating to go at him! Has he stayed away for fear he'll be vanquished?'

The crowd parted. The tension in the air made many hold their breath. The local expert arrived, swathed in a brilliant waist garment, his eyes dark with concentration. The conch blew loud and long, the drumming grew more and more vigorous.

The eighteenth round of combat began. The champion and the challenger threw themselves at each other, pirouetting and lunging, dodging and grunting, each testing the nuances of the eighteenth adavu. Just as the challenger seemed to be getting the better of him, the champion unwound the shining urumi from his waistband

and twirled it around his head fiercely. But his opponent, undaunted, drew out his own urumi doublequick. A smile of victory lurked in the challenger's eyes.

The sun was past its peak; it had begun its descent into the western horizon. Sensing that the combat would prove inconclusive once more, the champion decided to take the extreme step. He chanted the mantra under his breath. And before the startled eyes of the watchers-on, he turned into a magnificent tiger, his stripes rippling over his sleek muscles.

The chenda continued to drum at a frenzied pace. Not a single person uttered a word. The tiger leapt upon the challenger. Within minutes, his jaws dripping with blood, he left the remains of the defeated hero on the ground and strode away, disappearing into the groves that led to his village.

His wife had been preparing for his return all morning. She had prayed hard for her husband's victory. As she saw the tiger approaching through the grove, her heart danced with joy.

But as the tiger strode closer, she saw the fire in its red-tinged eyes, the blood dripping from its jaws. Panic-stricken at this fearsome sight, her feet turned to lead. Her hands trembled uncontrollably. She forgot to chant the mantra or reach for the cow dung water with her broomstick. With a shriek of utter terror, she fainted in a heap on the ground before the hut.

What happened to the tiger after that? He fled to the forest, where he lived out his remaining years, unable to regain his human form. But the villagers did not forget their hero. They still worship him as a god in human form or a Teyyam, whose spirit comes to life each year as Pulimaranha Tondachan, with peacock-bright headgear and a stiffened white skirt-like costume below his bare torso, a contrast to his black-painted face.

As the village children in northern Kerala watch him, surrounded by their elders, they have been known to say, 'That tiger never did die, after all. Did he?'

The Jackals and the Tiger

WILLIAM FREDERICK TRAVERS O'CONNOR

Once upon a time there was a family of Jackals, consisting of a Father, Mother, and five young ones. After living for some time very comfortably near a large village, they found that the dogs of the village were becoming so numerous and so troublesome that they considered it necessary to change their place of abode. So one fine evening they started off and travelled away across the country, keeping a sharp look-out for some desirable spot in which they might settle down.

After a while they came to the edge of a forest, and having travelled for some little distance into the thickest part of the wood, they arrived all of a sudden at a Tiger's den. The young Jackals were a good deal frightened at the smell of the Tiger's den, but Father Jackal reassured them, and said that he thoroughly understood Tigers, and knew how to deal with them. So he went forward alone, and, peeping in, he found that the Tiger was out, but that he had left a large quantity of deer's flesh lying in one corner, which apparently he had not had time to consume. So he called Mrs Jackal and the children, and told them to go inside and to have a good feed, and to make themselves quite comfortable. After making a good meal himself off the deer's flesh, he said to Mrs Jackal:

'You and the children can now go to sleep; I shall go on to the roof of the den and keep a look-out for the Tiger. When I see him coming I shall rap on the roof, and you must at once wake up the children and make them begin to cry, and when I ask you what they are crying about, you must say that they are getting impatient for their supper.'

Accordingly Mr Jackal went up on the roof, while his family settled down to sleep in the snuggest corner of the Tiger's den. Shortly after Father Jackal heard a slight crackling amongst the dry leaves of the forest; and in the dim morning light he discerned the form of a great Tiger approaching his den through the tree-stems.

According to the arrangement he had made, he rapped with a loose stone upon the roof of the den, and Mrs Jackal immediately woke up the young Jackals and made them cry.

'What are those children crying about?' called out Father Jackal.

'They are very hungry, and getting impatient for their supper,' was the reply.

'Tell them they won't have long to wait now,' said Father Jackal, ' the Tiger will probably be home very soon, and we shall all be eating hot Tiger's meat before long.'

On hearing this the Tiger was very much alarmed, and thought to himself:

'What kind of strange animal can this be which has entered my den, and is waiting to cook and eat me on my return; it must certainly be a very fierce and terrible creature.'

So without waiting to investigate the matter any further, he turned tail and ran off as fast as he could through the forest. After running some way, he came across an old Baboon, with a great fringe of white hair all round his face.

'Where are you running to, Uncle Tiger?' asked the Baboon.

'Well,' said the Tiger, 'the fact is, that a family of strange animals, who call themselves Jackals, are at this moment in occupation of my den. As I was approaching my den, after a long night's hunting, one of the creatures was actually sitting on the roof, looking out for me, and as I got close up I heard him tell his young ones that they were to have hot Tiger's meat for supper. Fortunately for me, he hadn't seen me, so I thought the best thing I could do was to make off as fast as I could, in order to avoid being eaten.'

On hearing this the Baboon was very much amused, and set to work to laugh very heartily.

'Why,' said he, 'what a foolish Tiger you are! Have you never heard of a Jackal before? Don't you know that it is you who should eat the Jackals, and not the Jackals you? You come along with me, and I will soon show you how to deal with people like that.'

The Tiger was somewhat reassured on hearing what the Baboon had to say, but, even so, he was at first very reluctant to return again and to incur the danger of being eaten; but the Monkey encouraged him, and finally they set off together, the Monkey twisting his tail round the Tiger's, in order to give him a feeling of support and confidence.

As they came nearer to the den, the Tiger grew more and more timorous, and would only advance very slowly, ready to take flight at any moment. However, they went on together, tail-in-tail, until presently Father Jackal on the roof of the den caught sight of the pair, and called out:

'That is right, Brother Monkey, bring him along quickly; we are all half starved. But what do you mean by only bringing one of them? I had expected you would bring us at least two or three.'

On hearing this, the Tiger at once suspected that the Baboon was in the Jackal's employ, and that he was being led into a trap. Without a moment's hesitation he turned about and fled precipitately into the depths of the forest. The unfortunate Baboon, whose tail was tightly twisted round the Tiger's, was unable to free himself, and was dragged and bumped hither and thither in the Tiger's rush through the thickest and thorniest parts of the jungle. When at length the Tiger paused, many miles away, to take breath, he looked back at his flanks, and all he saw of the Monkey was a bit of its tail which had broken off and was still twisted round his own.

He never again returned to his den, which was occupied henceforth by the Jackals, who lived there for many years in peace and comfort.

Padmini

VALMIK THAPAR

We were back in Delhi, the feel of the forest still with us, odd bite of information buzzing in our heads, waiting for our next opportunity, the call as it were. It came soon enough with the new year 1977. There was a ring at the doorbell of my house—a telegram for me, from Fateh Singh. 'Come immediately,' it said. It was a mad rush as Tejbir Singh and I organized ourselves to leave in the morning. We took the train and were met by an excited and jumpy Fateh at the other end. His first words (and I still remember them) were: 'A tigress has been spotted with five cubs.' Fateh Singh then spent some time explaining. His experience had begun several months ago when he first set eyes on the tigress, whom we now decided to name Padmini.

The year in which her story starts is 1976. Padmini was then a four-year-old tigress in the Ranthambhore Tiger Reserve of Rajasthan and Fateh Singh was the assistant field director, when he sighted her in a very pregnant state, her belly bulging hugely. This is cause for great excitement to any field man in a forest; a new lot of tiger cubs to be born.

Driving his jeep near the vacated Lakarda village on an evening in December 1976, he sighted some pugmarks. A careful examination of the tracks immediately revealed that a tigress was moving with a large brood—unbelievable in many ways and rare for any tiger reserve in India. A mother and five cubs! He could tell the approximate age from the size of the marks and was beside himself with excitement. Some time ago, this would have been the most unlikely place for the find. When still inhabited the noise of the cattle, the shouts and cries of men, women and children kept all the animals miles away. There was no possibility of shelter as all the grass and trees around had been destroyed by the villagers. But Lakarda was now deserted;

after the shift, the grass had come up slowly and nature had taken over the deserted settlement. Animal life moves freely in and around it now. It is here that we believe Padmini gave birth to her family.

An immediate problem was keeping track of the movement of the tigers for, so far, no satisfactory method has been evolved to do this. (An experiment was conducted in neighbouring Nepal to determine the movement of a tiger by collaring the animal. A collar with a transmitter attached to it emits signals which allow one to track the animal's movement. In India, this experiment was conducted on other animals such as the nilgais, cheetal and sambar, the first attempt with a tiger resulted in a casualty and the experiment was abandoned. Also, the major concern of Indian wildlife has been on keeping man's interference with the ecological system to forest down to a minimum.) Fateh's only recourse was to keep track the movements of the tigress by following her pugmarks and her kills by attempting to establish her territory and pinpoint her presence in different areas.

'As though aware that she was marked.' Padmini began a game of hide and seek with him, complicating an already difficult situation.

Although Fateh Singh had been seeing masses of fresh pugmarks—indications of a large family of tigers—no actual sighting had been made somehow. Padmini's excessive caution had to be broken down, and some kind of rapport developed between her and her human observers.

It was in early January 1977 that the tension was broken and Padmini first showed herself. Fateh was sitting in a hide near the village, hoping for some sign of the family which had been active in the area during the morning. It was twilight; the first stars were appearing in the sky. The crickets and the nightjars had started their chatter. An icy wind was blowing. Suddenly, the stillness of the night was shattered by the shrieking death cry of a buffalo. Immediately afterwards, a brooding silence enveloped the forest. Not a sound was heard in the dark.

Fateh moved off quickly towards the noise of the buffalo when the lights of the jeep caught Padmini head-on. Approximately nine feet in length, with a beautiful coat and in the best of health, she stared at him and snarled. Suddenly, in a flurry of movement, five young tigers ran across the road, disappearing into the bushy country around. It seemed as if the cubs had rushed into hiding on their mother's indication. Padmini watched Fateh carefully and with a measured tread walked away, leaving his heart beating faster at this first sighting of the complete brood. It was also the first sign of success after a patient wait of many days. The dawn brought Fateh back to the same area in the freezing cold. Early morning frost covered large stretches of the forest; his hands were numb driving the jeep, his eyes smarting with the chill, but there she was, at the spot of the night before, sitting over her prey. To her right lay a full-size lame buffalo which she had killed the night before. Only a portion from the hind legs had been eaten. None of her cubs were in sight. Padmini watched Fateh suspiciously. This was amazing behaviour for, during the day, tigers will normally find dense shelter to sleep in. But

Padmini sat alert—she was guarding the meat. She knew that every ounce mattered and she would have to keep continuous vigil to prevent it from being scavenged by vultures, jackals or hyenas. Because of the special situation her whole pattern of behaviour had undergone a change: she was spending the day alert instead of asleep.

At about mid-day when Fateh heard a jackal call from the left of the tree he realized that this was a definite sign that the cubs were moving towards their mother. The jackal alarm call is warning of the presence of a predator. Sure enough within ten minutes two cubs appeared under the tree. Fateh was unable to photograph them because of the awkward angle: the branches obstructed his vision. The tigress suddenly lifted her head and seemed to signal to her offspring, who vanished instantly. Once again the jackal called, after which silence prevailed. The tigress relaxed. During all this, Fateh had stuck to only observing the scene. Now, keeping a certain distance, he perched on the branch of a tree to keep watch and to photograph. On the first click of the camera, Padmini made a threatening charge, stopping directly under the branch where Fateh sat. For a brief moment, the thought of man and tiger confronting each other on the same branch crossed Fateh's mind. But tigers very rarely climb trees, unlike other members of the cat family. Secure in this knowledge, Fateh clicked on. Padmini charged again but half-heartedly, demonstrating the tremendous power that this magnificent animal is capable of. Convinced that the man on the tree meant no harm and confident of her own prowess, she seemed to be ignoring him. She snoozed, dozed, yawned, rolled over, nibbled the meat. The suspicion had worn off. It was as though she had started accepting his presence and was behaving naturally. For five days, from early morning to late evening, Fateh sat watching her, but all through she kept guard with no sign of her cubs, who obviously only came at night after he had left. The carcass of the buffalo slowly diminished and on the last day hardly anything was left, but she still sat guard. All her actions conformed to the needs of her cubs. Not an ounce of flesh was to be scavenged or wasted as long as her cubs could continue feeding on it undisturbed.

This is when we came into the picture, to add to the mounting excitement and tension. Were Padmini's young ones determined to remain invisible to us or were our efforts going to prove successful?

During the months of January and February we saw Padmini often. She was a picture of confidence and less and less bothered by our presence so long as we maintained a certain distance. The cubs kept out of sight but we were fortunate enough to get fleeting glimpses of them as they rushed by and scattered. But noticeably longer stretches of observation were possible each successive time as the cubs seemed to be more secure in our presence.

We were now able to distinguish between the sexes and found that Padmini had three male and two female cubs. But the real question was would Padmini manage to hunt and kill for herself as well as provide for growing tigers, and for how long? It was a mammoth task under any instances. An approximate idea of the total consumption of meat would be an excellent indication of the problems facing a tiger family. Padmini had to ensure an average to minimum consumption of sixty-five to eighty kilograms of meat every few days.

The young ones were of slightly different sizes. There was one dominant male cub, tougher and fitter than his brothers and sisters. He seemed more venturesome, confident and courageous, especially in our presence; we decided to name the male cubs, Akbar, Hamir and Babar.

The female cubs were more fragile: smaller than Akbar and a shade smaller than Babar and Hamir, they seemed definitely more delicate and feminine. There was a slight difference even between the two of them. The smallest, whom we called Begum, was not in the best of health and gave us some worry. During our first few glimpses, she was always lagging behind the rest of the family. Poor little Begum—she was part of a very natural phenomenon in the wild where the youngest in a family is totally dominated by her brothers and sisters. It was obvious that she was getting the smallest share of the meat after a kill and that she was the shyest, eating last of all. It was a sad situation and we were worried about her chances of survival.

The other female, whom we called Laxmi, was in much better condition but always one step behind her brothers.

Now that the entire family had been identified, the complex task of assimilating and analyzing the different behaviour patterns of each member began. Normally, much confusion could arise in studying such a large family and distinguishing one from the other. What is important to note is that Padmini, Akbar, Babar, Hamir, Laxmi and Begum all had different characteristics, facial expressions and most important of all, different markings. Tigers can be distinguished by the markings on their foreheads and around the sides of their faces. This is a sure method of recognition. After taking a series of photographs, it was possible to enlarge the face, study the pattern of stripes around the mouth and forehead and slowly be able to tell the difference between the members of the family. The stripes on the body also vary considerably.

Our worst suspicions regarding little Begum were confirmed during the last week of February. In the evening, we had spotted Padmini moving through the area and had decided to camp out on the incline in the hope of seeing some developments. This was an important area for water and we felt the family might come to drink before their siesta during the day. We had spent the night at an observation post in the hope of viewing the family in the early hours of the morning. It was a beautiful spot with patches of tall grass interspersed with shrubs, not thick enough to obstruct the vision and right below us was a dried riverbed next to which there was a waterhole. The family had been extremely active here; it was very close to Lakarda village where Padmini had first been sighted.

We woke up with the dawn. The birds had started their chatter; the morning was cold and crisp. We crept along the ground to the edge of the incline and looked below. And there they were: Padmini walking through the grass even before the first rays of the sun were out behind her, with Akbar, followed by Babar and Hamir and then Laxmi—but not a sign of little Begum. Had she got lost somewhere or was it possible that in the last week she had been unable to cope with the pressure of living and had given up and let nature take its course? We kept putting the thought out of our minds as we watched Padmini and her four young ones disappear into the forest. There was still a faint hope that Begum had strayed and might join them later. In any case, we decided that this was an important development and we must somehow confirm it. So, by evening, we tied a buffalo near Lakarda to study the pugmarks and view the family closely. The time was 5 p.m. When we returned around 11 p.m., the buffalo was dead and partly eaten. On hearing the sound of jeep, the family had moved away to a more secure position in the grass.

Using our powerful searchlight we identified Padmini sitting beside her female cub, Laxmi.

Nearby, with a slightly snarly expression on his face, sat dominant Akbar. A little behind were Babar and Hamir. Of little Begum there was no sign. What we feared had obviously happened, Little Begum was no more; nature had eased her out. She had been the littlest in the family and her health was affected by her position in the family hierarchy. She had not been able to get enough food and had probably just wasted away.

The Rise and Fall of the Emerald Tigers

RAGHU CHUNDAWAT

Lessons for young tigers start very early. It begins with play at an early age. Play with siblings and the mother is an important activity while growing up as they learn their basic lessons and establish hierarchies. Soon they move from playing with the mother's tail to exploring their immediate surroundings. As they grow, the cubs gain confidence. By the time they are over two-and-a-half months old, they will sometimes, though not always, accompany their mother to only kill. These are exciting times for the cubs. The mother will lead them to the carcass and sit down from where she can watch them.

It is the mother's call when to expose her cubs to observers like us. It varied with different litters. Initially, they were very hard to see, but then one day the mother would feel confident, give a few calls and one saw cubs coming out of nowhere. It can happen at any age, sometimes as early as three months, but in other cases it might not happen until five months.

Some cubs are bold and others very shy, irrespective of their sex. Each cub has an individual temperament that stays with them throughout their life. This diversity of traits is an important element in future survival. In Panna we found that they would slowly get used to our presence until we could watch them play, eat or sleep without any disturbance.

At five or six months the cubs are more confident of their surroundings. If they see prey they may stalk it for a while. In the fawning season—September to November is the peak in Panna—they may get early hunting lessons. Once Joanna saw F-120 catch a sambar fawn alive and leave it for the cubs. The cubs were barely six months old and seemed to have some vague instinct but no real clue how to kill it. The fawn was like a live toy on which they could practise their hunting skills. One of the cubs took complete possession of the fawn. By this time, hierarchies among the siblings are already established and on this occasion the dominant cub played with the unfortunate fawn until late in the evening and we had to leave as darkness was falling. On several occasions, I saw Baavan, F-120 and F-113 catch a chital fawn and carry it to the cubs, still alive. Once we saw Baavan carrying the fawn over a fairly long distance of one-and-a-half kilometres and by the time she arrived with the fawn it was half-dead. Both the cubs played with it for hours before eating it. Quite often during the fawning season, we observed older cubs (above twelve months) join their mothers to flush out and chase down fawns. This seems like good practice to develop their skills and gain confidence in hunting.

Over time the mother provides them with more difficult prey such as a large wild boar, leaving it for the cubs to handle. On one occasion, two fourteen-month-old cubs of Baavan struggled for over forty minutes handling a pig. This scene was completely chaotic, creating a lot of commotion, noise and dust as the inexperienced cubs tried their best to bring the pig down. The pig would escape their hold for a while, only to get caught again, and the struggle would continue. All this time the mother sat at a distance watching the ruckus in an apparently disinterested manner. However, once when it looked as though the pig was escaping out of the cubs range and they were just standing there in shock, she got up and caught it again in a flash. It was amazing how quick her response was. As soon as she caught the pig, the cubs were at it again. We watched this for over thirty minutes more from the back of an elephant, until it grew dark and we had to leave. We continued to hear the struggle for another fifteen minutes from the road.

On another occasion, a similar thing happened when we were tracking F-111 in the night. She was about forty metres in front of us, when we saw a big wild boar crossing the road towards her. She caught it as soon as it crossed the road, and then gave charge to her two seventeen-month-old cubs. This time it was already dark, so we could only hear what appeared to be the cries of the pig; it sounded similar to the brawl mentioned before. The mother moved several hundred metres away from the site. We left her and came back to where we could hear the commotion. This time, the struggle continued for an even longer time; we sat listening for two-and-a-half hours. When we returned in the morning the pig was half-eaten and we saw one of the cubs at the kill. Another arrived a little later but there was no sign of the mother. We finally located her a couple of kilometres away from the kill site. There were many other such observations showing how the mother created opportunities for the cubs to harness their predatory skills. This process starts at a very early age, though the cubs remain dependent on the mother until they are skilled predators. It is in the mother's interest that the cubs acquire these skills as early possible because the earlier they become independent, the sooner the mother is ready for her next litter.

We observed an instance of unusual behaviour between mother and cubs in Panna.

We saw F-120 teaching her last litter of cubs to climb trees. When her cubs were six or seven months old, she encouraged the cubs to follow her up a tree several times. She did this almost daily for a couple of weeks. She would climb onto the lower branches of a large tree such as a mahua and the cubs would try to follow. They would scramble at the trunk and when they somehow managed to reach her she would move along the branch, jump down and climb another tree. The cubs soon followed and tried again to climb the tree. We noticed this behaviour continue each afternoon for over two weeks. Sometimes, to our amazement, F-120 would climb fairly high branches. However, we observed only F-120 behaving in this way. None of her siblings or her mother were ever seen teaching tree-climbing to their cubs.

From an early age the cubs copy almost everything their mother does: scraping, spraying and claw-raking. They learn these means of communication to keep in touch with their mother and siblings—fairly quickly. By the time they are over a year old they tend to wander away from the mother and use their skills to navigate or to find a kill site. As they grow more confident, they move further away and keep in touch with the methods mentioned above. These short forays away from the mother, sometimes for several days, are the first steps towards becoming an adult.

‘I Want to Be a Man-eater’

RANJIT LAL

‘Just you see. I’m going to be a man-eater,’ Goonda, the two-month-old tiger cub declared, wrestling with a piece of chital gristle. His mother, Tania, had just brought in a fresh kill and now she lay some distance away watching her two cubs eat, her brandy-gold eyes shimmering.

‘Don’t be such a dork,’ his sister, Guddi, retorted tartly, closing her eyes in bliss as she bit into a piece of fresh liver. She glanced at her brother and grinned to herself. He really was such a dork, always in such a hurry to eat as much as he could that he rarely distinguished between the choice cuts of meat and the gristly bits and hard to crack bones. ‘You know what Mama said about that. Besides, eww... humans smell disgusting, can you imagine what they must taste like?’

'I don't care. Once I become a man-eater, they'll all be scared of me.'

'You think. They'll come after you with guns and that will be that.'

A little distance away, the waterhole gleamed, its pleated emerald green waters surrounded by high chalky cliffs. It was a favourite spot for the little tiger family: in fact, Tania had given birth to her cubs in one of the caves high up in the cliff face. She had scoped out a couple of more dens nearby too, just in case they needed to move in a hurry.

'Mama, this chital is really so tough,' Goonda complained. 'His skin is like a rhino's. He must have been a real old grandpa. Weren't there any softer ones available?'

Guddi grinned. 'Mama, ignore him. It is really delicious.'

'Just eat it,' Tania growled softly and glanced around, but the jungle seemed to be at peace. A few tree-pies hung around hopefully up in the nearby trees, calling to each other.

'Just wait until I make my first human kill and see if I share it with you,' Goonda went on. 'You can roll back on your tummy all you want, but hah! See if I give you any.'

His mother got up and walked up and cuffed him affectionately. 'Beta jaan, you are not going to be a man-eater, not now, not ever. How many times have I told you: humans spell trouble.'

Her lovely brandy eyes turned frosty. She knew she was both right and wrong about that. A shudder ran through her as she recalled that terrible night, some months ago.

A truck, with headlights blazing, had come careening around the bend just as she had begun crossing the forest road. It sent her flying into the ditch by the roadside, bleeding and battered. She had moaned with pain and fallen unconscious.

~

Tania was found by an anti-poaching patrol the next morning. They sedated her further, just to make sure she didn't awake while they took her back to the Park headquarters, where a message had already been sent. The Field Director of Tiger Falls National Park, Mr D.P.

Singhania, had radioed for a vet to be sent over from the district headquarters at the earliest.

The tigress was a sad sight when they laid her out on the table in what was called the 'Treatment Room', where all kinds of injured animals (usually due to road accidents) were brought. Her head was a bloody mess, and a shoulder seemed dislocated. Already flies had laid eggs in her open head wound.

'Will she be all right, Papa?' Twelve-year old Jyotsna asked her father as she stared horrified at the bloody mess of a once magnificent tigress. The vet, kindly Dr Ghosh, slipped an IV into the unconscious tigress and bent over her. Jyotsna was a pale-complexioned slip of a girl with a mass of brown curls and laughing brown eyes. 'Poor thing. She must be hurting so much.'

Jyotsna, too, knew a thing or two about hurting and hospitals and needles and drips and the tubes they put into you and blood they sucked out of you and stuff like that. She'd been awfully ill for the last two years, though they never told her exactly with what, just that her tummy and insides were not working properly, which was why she felt so sick and was never hungry. But she had recovered and come home, to Tiger Falls, where with fresh air, good food and being hugely fussed over by her father and his staff she had got well. So well, that she had even inveigled her father's official Gypsy driver, grizzled old Hari Singh, to teach her how to drive the Gypsy, without of course her father knowing anything about it.

Dr Ghosh looked at her and smiled. 'I think she'll be all right. We'll have to keep her here for a while under observation. I'll just set her shoulder and clean and sew up her head wound. She was lucky that no bones were broken.'

To Jyotsna she didn't look lucky at all. Dr Ghosh turned to the Field Director. 'If she recovers well enough you could release her back in the forest. She's expecting a litter very soon and it would be better if the cubs were born in the wild.' He looked relieved. 'I've checked. They seem to be all right.'

Tania was one furious tigress when she awoke. For a start she didn't understand what had happened to her. Her eyes blazed and she snarled viciously and swiped at the bars of the cage in which she had been kept—it was enough to make the bravest soul want to rush to the washroom. She was in pain, confused and very, very angry. The cage was actually quite big, but partitioned into two. Whenever they needed to clean it, they would open one section, tempt the tigress into it with a chunk of meat, close it and then clean the empty section: just as they do in some zoos.

From the doorway of the Treatment Room, Jyotsna stood calmly and listened to her. They had dropped a curtain in front of the cage bars, so as to (hopefully) calm the furious tigress down, but it didn't seem to help.

In the brief periods of silence between the snarls and the growls, Joystna spoke to her in her soft, gentle voice, full of what she felt for the wounded tigress.

'It's all right. I know how you feel. Don't worry. Dr Ghosh is the best. You'll be out of here before you know it.' It was exactly what so many nurses and doctors had told her in the hospital and they had been right, hadn't they?

'You just relax, girl. Papa's ordering a nice big fat buffalo for you.' Every second day, the staff would feed Tania huge chunks of meat (initially stuffed with medication), besides changing her water every day.

Her father had looked in on Jyotsna the first time she had talked to the tigress and smiled. 'Just don't go any closer to her. She'd like to take a swipe at you. Stay at the doorstep. No closer!'

'Papa, she's just scared and doesn't understand what's happened. I'm just trying to explain it to her.'

And so, for the most part all Tania heard was the soft, sweet voice emerging from somewhere beyond the curtain, not only talking to her but singing too. It soothed the tempestuous tigress down. And then one day they removed the curtain. Afraid again, Tania whipped up and down the cage like a flaming dervish snarling and agitated, but she calmed down as Jyotsna leaned against the doorway and spoke to her.

'You are looking so much better, you know. You were a real mess when you got here. You'd better thank Dr Ghosh for his good work. You hear me, girl?'

Tania did and let out another blood-curdling snarl.

'Okay, okay I get it. I felt like that when I was in hospital, too. You want to be out of that cage, right? So would I. It won't be long, just have a little patience. Now what would you like to hear me sing to you?' Jyotsna's eyes twinkled mischievously. 'Would you like me to sing, "Soft kitty, warm kitty, purr, purr purr"? It's from the *Big Bang Theory*, though I don't think you would have seen that. But anyway, here goes.'

And so, she sang it, and the agitated tigress closed her eyes.

Jyotsna talked to the tigress every single day that she was there, spending most of her time with the animal. She sat herself down comfortably on a chair near the door (just in case) and told her the stories her father had told her: about the exploits of Jim Corbett and Kenneth Anderson ('such a windbag, that fellow') and the maharajas and the British who hunted them in such a cowardly manner from the top of elephants and machans. 'And imagine, that silly fellow Kipling even made you the villain of his famous *Jungle Book*.

'I'm really so sorry for all those things,' she told the tigress. 'We nearly killed off all of you.' She rolled her eyes. 'And can you imagine in places like China they think that eating parts of you will help them behave like supermen and have more babies? Huh. As if we need any more.'

Then her brown eyes sparkled. 'Dr Ghosh said you're going to have babies. So, who's your boyfriend? Is he big and handsome? Must be, because you are really beautiful. Does he tell you that?'

Tania *was* beautiful. She was sleek and sinuous and as she mended, her coat glowed orange-gold, the black flames rippling as she moved fluidly up and down her cage.

And when Jyotsna started singing, the tigress would often close her eyes and doze peacefully. The little girl's voice was so magical and melodious that on several occasions the fierce tigress felt a purr rising within her; like a thrumming heavy-duty motor.

They let Tania out a little over a month after her accident. Of course, Jyotsna accompanied the release team. They sat in the Gypsy and watched as the cage door was opened and the tigress leapt out in a blaze of gold, vanishing into the forest. They had wanted to fit her with a radio-collar before freeing her, but the one they had obtained had malfunctioned right from the beginning, so they gave up the idea. But soon the forest guards reported that the tigress was often to be seen at the Emerald Waterhole; it was a perfect place for an ambush and also to relax in after a hunt and a meal. She seemed to have recovered completely.

So, that's where Jyotsna went with Hari Singh, whenever he was free to take her and waited quietly in the Gypsy for the tigress to make an appearance. Then suddenly, the tigress seemed to have vanished.

'She's probably had her cubs,' Hari Singh told her. 'If she is around here, she'll bring them out in a couple of months or so.'

Early one morning they got news that the tigress indeed had been spotted again at

Emerald Waterhole and Jyotsna wanted to rush there immediately. But there was a problem. The Deputy Director had picked up her father and the two had gone off to the district headquarters for an important meeting. Worse, Hari Singh was on leave. The other forest guards had gone on patrol because there was a tip-off regarding poachers being spotted at one corner of the park.

But the Gypsy was free...standing quietly in its shed. There was no one around. So, Jyotsna took the keys and drove quietly to the waterhole—around ten kilometres away. For a while, she just sat in the Gypsy and looked at the water. Then, knowing she was breaking a very big rule, she got out of the vehicle, and walked to the water's edge and sat down on a rock, watching a turquoise kingfisher dive into the water from time to time and a golden oriole coming down to drink. It didn't seem as if Tania was around. A covey of grey francolin (partridges) lined up to drink at the water's edge. Suddenly they perked up their heads and sauntered off hurriedly into the forest.

And then from across the waterhole, the reeds and rushes suddenly seemed to be agitated. Jyotsna stared hard and drew in her breath sharply. The reeds parted, rather like a theatre curtain opening before a show and the most gorgeous, orange and black tiger cub swaggered out, looking slightly drunk it had to be said, his white whiskers twitching, his jade green eyes fixed on her.

~

Jyotsna didn't know it, but she had been spotted by Goonda and Guddi from their cave hideout as soon as she had driven up. And then she had gotten out of the vehicle...

'Hah. There's my first human kill,' Goonda told his sister as he stared at the little girl across the water. 'Watch me. I'll rend her limb from limb.'

'Don't be such an idiot. She's already seen you,' Guddi said. 'You think she's going to hang around for you to pounce on her? She'll scream and run any minute.' She looked behind her. 'I wish Mama would come back. She'll teach you.

She's going to have such a fit.' Their mother had gone off on yet another hunt.

'Watch and learn, sis, watch and learn. I'll just hypnotize her with a look. She'll freeze with fear.'

But unfortunately for Goonda, Jyotsna did not seem to freeze with terror. She seemed utterly enchanted and entranced. So enchanted that she had forgotten the golden rule of survival in the jungle: *never* get between a mother (of any kind) and her cubs. And the cubs' mom was sure to be around somewhere close.

'Hello,' she said softly. 'Wow, you are a handsome little dude, aren't you. And is that your sister behind you? She's so pretty!' Her brown eyes widened. 'Ah, are you trying to stalk me?' she asked amusedly.

Across the waterhole, Goonda froze. His green eyes—killer eyes, he believed—glittered. His ears went back and he tried to control his tail madly snaking this way and that. He fixed his eyes on Jyotsna and took a step forward, then another. And tripped over a rock, landing flat on his chin with a thump. 'Oof!' he snorted as the air went out of him. Dust went up his nose and he sneezed. He looked a little goofy.

Jyotsna giggled. 'Ooh, you silly fellow. I hope you didn't hurt yourself. But you'll never catch anything if you keep falling over.'

Goonda's ears pricked up. That voice. Surely, he had heard it somewhere earlier. Dimly perhaps, and he couldn't remember when, but definitely. He turned around to look at Guddi. She now had a sweet, melting look on her face. Really, girls were so silly.

But hey, a man-eating tiger cub's gotta do what a man-eating tiger cub's gotta do. He resumed skirting the waterhole, crouching low to the ground and creeping forward step by step as he had seen his mother do. Behind him Guddi followed him, mewling her protestations.

'You know, I used to sing "Soft kitty...warm kitty, little ball of fur." to your mom, when she was sick,' Jyotsna said and started doing just that.

This time poor Goonda just turned into a puddle straightaway. He waddled up to the little girl and rubbed his furry head against her calves. Not to be left behind, Guddi joined him. Jyotsna gasped in delight as she picked them up turn by turn and hugged them. It was utterly disgraceful: instead of behaving like spitfires and hellcats, the cubs were behaving like puddy-tats. And it was all the fault of that lovely, becalming voice...

But at the back of Jyotsna's mind a warning light was flashing now. Just what did she think she was doing? Playing with these gorgeous tiger cubs, when their mother could make an appearance any moment and make mincemeat out of her...

And the mother was indeed racing towards the waterhole right at that moment. A snarl of sheer fury began rising in Tania's throat as she bounded up. Then, concealed by the reeds and rushes, she crouched down, preparing to leap at the human who had dared to touch and caress her babies.

She took in the scene before her. Her two incorrigible brats were playing with that little girl who had once not long ago sung to her and soothed her when she had been frightened, in pain and confused. As she was now doing to her cubs. The fire died from the tigress's blazing eyes. A deep rumbling purr arose in her throat as she settled down and watched...

P.S.: Oh yes, Goonda and Guddi both got a spanking afterwards but it was not a spanking that seemed to hurt them at all. 'You little charmer,' Tania growled softly as she gently cuffed her little son, 'You are not going to be any man-eater. More likely a lady-killer.'

P.P.S.: You really really should NEVER think of doing what Jyotsna did!

The Tigress

PRATHIBHA NANDAKUMAR

He is the animal trainer
makes even the fiercest of fierce animals
crawl, jump, stand on hind legs
just by the crack of his whip.

He puts his head between
the dangerous teeth of the tiger
pats his appreciation
waits in anticipation
of applause.

This tigress
that roamed the deep jungle,
terror of the forest,
now sits cross-legged in front of him.
Is she a tigress or what?

Someone once asked her about it.
She just smiled and brought out
her long sharp nails
hidden well under her paws
and scratched her head.

About the Authors

Zai Whitaker grew up in a family of naturalists in Mumbai, and moved to Chennai in 1974 when she married Rom Whitaker and joined his work at the Madras Snake Park. Together, they started the Madras Crocodile Bank in 1976, and several other conservation projects focused on reptile conservation. She has worked closely with the Irular tribe of snake catchers and her recent book, *Termite Fry*, is based on their lives and history. She has written twenty books, mostly for children, on nature and the environment. She is currently the Managing Trustee of the Crocodile Bank.

Hugh Allen served in the British Armed Forces during the Second World War but, when a bad head wound put him out of active service in 1942, he was hospitalized in India. He learnt to love the country and took up farming amongst the jungles, developing his skills for big-game shooting out of necessity, rather than entertainment.

Dhan Gopal Mukherji grew up in Bengal, before he moved to Japan and then the United States. In the US he started his writing career and went on to win much acclaim for his books. He wrote a number of books for children, including the prestigious Newbery Medal-winning *Gay-Neck, the Story of a Pigeon* (1927). His children's books include *Kari the Elephant*, *Hari the Jungle Lad*, *Ghond the Hunter*, *Hindu Fables*, *Fierce Face*, among others. Read his books *Fierce-Face the Tiger*, *The Adventures of Sirdar* and *The Cat Who Became King* in Talking Cub.

Ruskin Bond is the author of numerous novels, novellas, short-story collections and non-fiction books, many of them classics. Among them are *When I Was a Boy*, *Lone Fox Dancing*, *The Room on the Roof*, *A Flight of Pigeons*, and *A Book of Simple Living*. He received the Sahitya Akademi Award in 1993, the Padma Shri in 1999 and the Padma Bhushan in 2014.

Jim Corbett, or Edward James Corbett, was an Indian-born British hunter, tracker, naturalist, and author who hunted a number of man-eating tigers and leopards in the Indian subcontinent. He authored *Man-Eaters of Kumaon*, *Jungle Lore*, and other books recounting his hunts and experiences, which enjoyed critical acclaim and commercial success. He became an avid photographer and spoke out for the need to protect India's wildlife from extermination.

William Blake was an English poet, painter, and printmaker. Largely unrecognized during his lifetime, Blake's work is today considered seminal and significant in the history of both poetry and the visual arts. Blake is highly regarded for his expressiveness and creativity, and the philosophical and mystical currents that underlie his work.

Ruth Plumly Thompson was an American writer of children's stories, best known for writing many novels placed in Oz, the fictional land of L. Frank Baum's classic children's novel *The Wonderful Wizard of Oz* and its sequels.

Anjana Basu works as an advertising consultant in Kolkata. She writes stories and features in the local newspapers and for *Outlook* and *Statesman*. She is the author of a number of novels, children's books and short story collections. Some of her books for children include *Grandfather's Tiger Tales*, *In the Shadow of the Leaves*, *Leopard in the Laboratory*,

Eighteen Tides and a Tiger, Hide and Seek Tiger, Lockdown Tiger and *Chinku and the Wolfboy.*

William Frederick Travers O'Connor was an Irish diplomat and officer in the British and British Indian armies. He is remembered for his travels in Asia, cartography, study and publication of local cultures and language, particularly about Tibet.

James McIntyre was a Scottish poet who emigrated to Canada in 1851. He is sometimes called The Cheese Poet, as cheese was a recurring theme in many of his poems.

Sunity Devi was the Maharani of the princely state of Cooch Behar in British India. She was an educationalist and a women's rights activist at heart. She wrote *The Beautiful Mogul Princesses* (1918), *Bengal Dacoits and Tigers* (1916), and *The Life of Princess Yashodara: Wife and Disciple of the Lord Buddha* (1929).

Bulbul Sharma is a writer and an artist. She teaches art to children with special needs. She is the author of a number of books for adults and children. She lives mostly in the hills where she loves going on bird-watching and talking-to-trees excursions.

S. Eardley-Wilmot was a British civil servant, forestry officer and conservationist who worked primarily in India and Burma and served as Inspector-General of Forests.

Flora Annie Steel was an English writer who was fascinated by Indian culture and spent twenty-two years in British India, writing extensively about the stories she heard and her own experiences in the country as the outspoken and critical wife of an engineer in the Indian Civil Service. Steel was described as 'the female Rudyard Kipling' and was noted especially for books set in India for both adults and children, particularly a book on housekeeping in India for Englishwomen, *The Adventures of Akbar* and *Tales of the Punjab*, as well as novels and short stories.

Ella Wheeler Wilcox was an American author and poet. Wilcox was an advocate of animal rights and vegetarianism. Her works include the collection *Poems of Passion* and the poem 'Solitude', which contains the famous lines 'Laugh, and the world laughs with you; weep, and you weep alone.'

Aditi De is a Bangalore-based author, dreamer, traveller, editor (though not necessarily in that order). She loves children and the world of the word. In 1989, she launched *Junior Quest*, the popular magazine from the Chandamama group, and later edited the *Open Sesame* children's supplement at the *Deccan Herald*. Her books include A *Twist in the Tale: More Indian Folktales* (Puffin India). She has written children's columns for Chatterbox magazine, *Deccan Chronicle* and *Young World*.

Valmik Thapar has spent several decades serving the wild tigers of India. During this time, he has written more than twenty books and made or presented nearly a dozen films for the BBC and several other television networks on the tiger and Indian flora and fauna. He has also created a major non-governmental organization dedicated to conserving wildlife, the Ranthambhore Foundation. He campaigns and fights for new ways to save wild tigers and nature in India.

Raghu Chundawat is a renowned conservation biologist whose main studies have been on snow leopards and tigers. His pioneering ten-year research on the Panna tigers was immortalized in the BBC documentary, *Tigers of the Emerald Forest*.

Ranjit Lal is the author of forty-five books—fiction and non-fiction—for children and adults who are children. His abiding interest in natural history, birds, animals and insects is reflected in many of his books: *The Little Ninja Sparrows*, *Owlet*, *Not Out*, *The Harmony of Bees and Other Charms of Creepy Crawlies* and others. His other books with social themes include *Faces in the Water*, *Our Nana Was a Nutcase*, *Taklu and Shroom*, *Miracles*, *Smitten*, *The Secret of Falcon Heights*, *The Dugong and the Barracudas* and *The Battle for* No. 19. He enjoys photography, reading and cooking. He lives in Delhi.

Prathibha Nandakumar is an Indian poet, journalist, feminist, columnist and activist who works in Kannada and English. She is considered to be one of the pioneers of modern woman's poetry in Kannada literature. For her work *Kavadeyaata*, Pratibha was awarded the Karnataka Sahitya Akademi Award for Poetry in 1998.

Acknowledgements

Grateful acknowledgement is made to the following for permission to reprint copyright material:

Ruskin Bond for 'Timothy' and 'To See a Tiger'.

'Tiger, Tiger Who Are You' from *A Twist in the Tale* by Aditi De; Puffin; 2005, used with permission from Penguin Random House India.

Valmik Thapar for 'Padmini'.

Raghu Chundawat for the excerpt from *The Rise and Fall of the Emerald Tigers* (Speaking Tiger, 2018).

Prathibha Nandakumar for 'The Tigress'.

~

'Drought-stricken Land' excerpted from *Fierce-Face the Tiger*

'The Hungry Tiger of Oz' excerpted from *The Hungry Tiger of Oz*

'The Art of Hunting' excerpted from *Ghond the Hunter*

'The Palki and the Tiger' excerpted from *Bengal Tigers and Dacoits*

'The Home of the Tiger' excerpted from *Life of a Tiger*

'The Foolish Tiger' excerpted from *Tales of the Punjab*

~

Image on page vii *Tiger Walking* by Antoine-Louis Barye
Image on page 60 *Die Gartenlaube* by various
Image on page 126 *Tiger, from the Animals of the World Series* (T180) issued by Abdul Cigarettes
Image on page 221, A *performer wrestling with a trained tiger*, Wellcome Images